FOOTBALL
Quiz Book

FOOTBALL

Quiz Book

STOPWATCH

Published by Stopwatch Publishing Limited
For Bookmart Limited
Registered Number 2372865
Trading as Bookmart Limited
Desford Road
Enderby
Leicester
LE9 5AD

This edition published 1997

Printed and bound in Great Britain

Compiled by Jay Bigwood and with thanks to staff at Hayters Sports
Agency

© Stopwatch Publishing Limited
443 Oxford Street
London W1R 1DA

ISBN 1 90003291 0

CONTENTS

Quiz 1 — The Football League

1. **Which 12 teams were the founder members of the Football League?**

2. Who won the first ever Football League title?

3. **With what club did Billy Southworth score the first ever double hat-trick in 1893?**

4. Which team won the first title of the Twentieth Century?

5. **Who won the league for the second year running, in 1903-04, by scoring 48 goals, one fewer than Liverpool who were relegated?**

6. Which team set a record of 14 straight league victories in the First Division, in the 1903-04 season?

7. **For which side did 22 stone Bill "Fatty" Foulke sign in the 1904-05 season?**

8. Which team won 14 consecutive matches in the second division in 1905-06 to set a record?

9. **With which club did Alf Common sign to become the first £1000 player in 1905?**

10. Who were the first southern club to lead the First Division in the 1906-07 season?

11. **For which London team did George Hilsdon score five goals on his debut in the 1906-07 season?**

12. For which Midlands team did West, Hooper and Spouncer all score hat-tricks in a 12-0 win over Leicester Fosse in 1909?

13. **Which team lost 9-1 to Sunderland in the 1908-09 season, yet still managed to win the First Division?**

14. In which season did Manchester United first play at Old Trafford?

15. **Which team scored 36 out of a possible 42 points in their last 21 games to secure promotion in the 1909-10 season?**

---

1. **Preston North End, Villa, Wolves, Blackburn, Bolton, WBA, Accrington, Everton, Burnley, Derby, Notts County, Stoke** 2. Preston North End 3. **Everton** 4. Liverpool 5. **Sheffield Wednesday** 6. Manchester United 7. **Chelsea** 8. Bristol City 9. **Middlesbrough** 10. Woolwich Arsenal 11. **Chelsea** 12. Nottingham Forest 13. **Newcastle United** 14. 1910-11 15. **Oldham.**

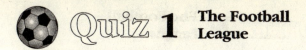

16. Who won their sixth League title in the 1909-10 season?

17. **In which season did the League first pay money to the clubs finishing in the top places in the First Division?**

18. Before 1985, when was the last time that Tottenham beat Liverpool in the league at Anfield?

19. **In which season did Arsenal play their first League game at Highbury?**

20. Which team won the championship on only 46 points in 1915, the lowest total since the league was expanded to 20 teams in 1905?

21. **Which team scored a record 104 goals in their 1919-20 championship winning season?**

22. From which team did Leeds United take over Elland Road to play their home matches?

23. **Which team only managed to attract 13 spectators in their final home game of the 1920-21 season, after they were already relegated from the Second Division?**

24. Which club set a record when they went 42 League matches unbeaten from November 1977 to December 1978?

25. **For which team did Jimmy Evans become the first full back to be his side's top scorer, after scoring 10 penalties in the 1921-22 season?**

26. Which team finished the 1922-23 season with 42 points from 42 matches, 14 wins, 14 draws and 14 defeats, with 40 goals for and 40 goals against?

27. **For which team did Billy Smith score the first ever goal direct form a corner, in the 1924-25 season?**

28. Up to the start of the 1997-98 season, two clubs share the record of 29 unbetane League games from the start of a season. Who are they?

29. **Which teams competed in the first League match to have been broadcast on radio, on January 22 1927?**

30. Which team paid Stockport County three freezers full of ice cream for a player in the 1926-27 season?

16. Aston Villa. 17. 1910-11. 18. 1911-12. 19. 1913-14. 20. Everton. 21. West Bromwich Albion. 22. Leeds City. 23. Stockport. 24. Nottingham Forest. 25. Southend. 26. Southampton. 27. Huddersfield. 28. Leeds (1973-74), Liverpool (1987-88). 29. Arsenal and Sheffield United. 30. Manchester United.

Quiz 1 — The Football League

31. **Who scored nine goals in the last three matches of the 1927-28 season, to set a record of 60, which included 40 headers?**

32. For which team did Jimmy McGrory score 49 goals in 33 games and eight in a 9-0 win over Dunfermline in the late 1920s?

33. **Which club in the 1927-28 season was relegated with 38 points, the highest total for a club to go down, and were only 3 points behind Arsenal, 12 places above them?**

34. Which London club won the Third Division South in the 1927-28 season with a record 127 goals?

35. **In what year did numbers first appear on players' shirts in League matches?**

36. How old was Albert Geldard when he became the youngest league player, making his debut for Second Division Bradford Park Avenue in 1929 season?

37. **Which team finished runners-up in the Third Division South every year for six consecutive years in the 1920s?**

38. Which team won the First Division three years in a row, from 1923 to 1925, and finished runners-up for the next two years?

39. **Which team lost their first twelve games of the 1930-31 season?**

40. Who were the first team to leave the League in mid season, when they retired after six games in the 1931-32 season?

41. **With which team did Stanley Matthews make his League debut in the 1931-32 season?**

42. Which club was fined £250 for fielding understrength teams in the 1935-36 season?

43. **Which clubs played in the first televised League game, in August 1936?**

44. Which British club first signed an Argentinian, in 1937?

45. **In what League season was the arc at the front of the penalty area introduced?**

31. Dixie Dean 32. Celtic **33. Tottenham** 34. Millwall 35. 1928 36. 15 years 158 days **37. Plymouth** 38. Huddersfield **39. Manchester United** 40. Wigan Borough **41. Stoke** 42. Arsenal **43. Arsenal and Everton** 44. Barrow **45. 1937-**.

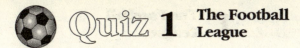

46. When was the offside rule brought in to League football?

47. For which club did Len Shackleton score six goals on his debut in the 1946-47 season?

48. For which club did 52 year old Neil McBain become the oldest man to play in the League in the 1946-47 season?

49. In what season did the League's aggregate attendance reach its highest ever figure - over 41.2 million?

50. In what season was obstruction made an offence in League football?

51. For which club did father and son Alec and David Herd both play in 1951?

52. Tommy Lawton scored his 200th League goal on the opening day of which season

53. For which club did Peter Aldis score a 35 yard header, thought to be the longest ever, in the 1952-53 season?

54. Who signed 34 year old Tommy Lawton in the 1953-54 season?

55. For which club did Sam Bartram set a League record of 500 appearances in March 1954?

56. Who set a League record of 401 consecutive games for Tranmere before missing a match in September 1955?

57. In what year did the first League game to use floodlights occur?

58. Who, in the 1956-57 season, set a League record of 30 games without a win?

59. Who scored 10 times for Luton Town against Bristol Rovers in a Division Three (South) match in 1936?

60. In what season did the Football League introduce a national Fourth Division?

46. 1925 47. **Newcastle** 48. New Brighton 49. 1948-49 50. 1948-49 51. Stockport 52. 1951-52 53. Aston Villa 54. Arsenal 55. **Charlton** 56. Harold Bell 57. 1956 58. Scunthorpe United 59. **Joe Payne** 60. 1958-59

Quiz 1 — The Football League

61. **In what year were Sunderland relegated to the Second Division for the first time since being formed in 1890?**

62. Which team beat Everton 10-4 in the 1958-59 season - the highest scoring First Division match this Century?

63. **Who became the youngest player to score five goals in a First Division match in 1958?**

64. Who reached 200 League goals in fewer matches than any other player, whilst playing for Middlesbrough in the 1950s?

65. **Who scored 59 goals in 37 League matches for Middlesbrough in 1926-27?**

66. Who led the PFA in their argument with the Football League over players' wages and contracts during the 1960-61 season?

67. **Which team won the 1962-63 championship and were labelled the "Cheque Book Champions"?**

68. Who retired in the 1963-64 season, aged 39, after making a record 764 appearances for Portsmouth?

69. **Who scored the fastest League goal in history in 1964, timed at 4 seconds, for Bradford Park Avenue?**

70. Who was the oldest player to have appeared in the First Division, aged 50 years and 5 days, in 1965?

71. **Keith Peacock become the first substitute to appear in a League match in 1965. Which club was he playing for at the time?**

72. Who scored 44 goals in the Fourth Division for Bradford Park Avenue in the 1965-66 season?

73. **Who took over at Hartlepools United to become the youngest manger in the League in 1966?**

74. In which season did all of the top three First Division clubs score over a hundred League goals?

75. **In what League season were goalkeepers limited to only four steps when holding the ball?**

61. 1958 62. Tottenham 63. **Jimmy Greaves** 64. Brian Clough 65. **George Camsell** 66. Jimmy Hill 67. **Everton** 68. Jimmy Dickinson 69. **Jim Fryatt** 70. Sir Stanley Matthews 71. **Charlton** 72. Kevin Hector 73. **Brian Clough** 74. 1930-31 75. 1967-68

76. How many goals did Tottenham score when they won the 1960-61 First Division?

77. **Who scored one of his six goals against Sunderland with his hand in October 1968?**

78. Who scored his 200th League goal for his First Division club in November 1968?

79. **Which team went from the Fourth Division to the First Division and back to the Fourth division in nine years?**

80. Who were fined a record £5,000 for fielding an understrength team in 1970?

81. **In what year were Blackpool last in the top division?**

82. Which club had to name their Chief Scout on the substitute's bench, in September 1970, because of a depleted squad?

83. **Who made his 500th League appearance for Chelsea in January 1970?**

84. Which club drew a record 23 out of 42 First Division matches in the First Division in the 1978-79 season?

85. **Which club won 18 of their 21 away League matches in Division Three (South) in 1946-47?**

86. Who scored 52 League goals in 1960-61 for Peterborough United?

87. **Who made his 600th appearance for Leeds in 1972?**

88. Which clubs was involved in match fixing allegations, for the match which decided the title, in 1972?

89. **Who replaced an injured linesman in a game between Arsenal and Liverpool in 1972?**

90. When did the distinction between amateur and professional footballers cease to exist in the League?

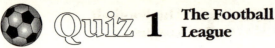
91. **Who was banned for life following a match fixing scandal, only to resume playing for Sheffield Wednesday in the 1972-73 season?**

92. In which year were Huddersfield relegated to the (old) Third Division for the first time in their history?

93. **Which two clubs were promoted from the Second to the First Division in 1972?**

94. Who were the Second Division champions in the 1961-62 season?

95. **Which club was promoted to the First Division in 1964 and ended up as runners-up the following year?**

96. In what year did Celtic win their ninth successive Scottish championship?

97. **In what year did Kilmarnock win their only Scottish First Division title?**

98. Which team set a record with eight scorers in one match during a First Division game in September 1989?

99. **Which club became the first to play 3,000 matches in the League, in 1975, and 3,500 in 1987?**

100. Which season saw the switching from goal average to goal difference in the Football League?

101. **Which Liverpool striker scored in 10 successive First Division matches from the last game of the 1986-87 season to the ninth of 1987-88?**

102. Who became the first English club to wear advertising on their shirts in the 1975-76 season?

103. **Which team was promoted to the Second Division in 1976, in only their fourth season in the Football League?**

104. Which club asked their fans to sponsor them at the start of the 1976-7 season?

105. **In which year were red and yellow cards introduced?**

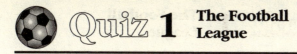

106. Which two players reached the 770 match mark for Chelsea on the same day in 1978?

107. Who became the first player to reach 100 League appearances for four different clubs?

108. Which club was first to legally wear a sponsor's name on their shirts?

109. Which club was relegated from the First Division alongside Norwich in 1974?

110. In what year did the Football League introduce three points for a win?

111. In what year was the sending off of players for "professional fouls" introduced?

112. In what year did Robert Maxwell become chairman of Oxford United

113. In what year did the League sign a deal which led to the League Cup being renamed the Milk Cup?

114. Who became the youngest First Division scorer, aged 16 years 57 days in February 1984?

115. Who finished bottom of the First Division in 1984-85, winning only three games and scoring a record low of 24 goals?

116. Who was First Division top scorer six times in 11 seasons - between 1958 and 1969?

117. Who was the youngest hat-trick scorer in the First Division, at the age of 17 years and 140 days, in 1988?

118. When was the last year that Brighton and Hove Albion were in the top division?

119. When did Portsmouth last win the championship?

120. When did Burnley last win the old First Division?

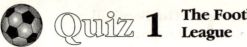

121. Who were the runners-up when the new First Division came into operation?

122. Who were the first new Third Division champions?

123. At the end of what League season did Ian Rush and Gary Lineker both move abroad?

124. In what season did Wimbledon first reach the top division?

125. When did Kenny Dalglish score his 100th League goal for Liverpool?

126. Who scored 37 League hat-tricks for Tranmere and Everton between 1924 and 1938?

127. Who did Arsenal beat on September 8 1984 to put them top of the First Division for the first time since 1972?

128. Which team recovered from a 4-0 half time deficit at Portsmouth to draw the match 4-4, in the Second Division, on New Year's Day, 1984?

129. Which club was relegated from the First Division to the Fourth Division in four straight seasons from 1983-84?

130. Which club postponed two matches in October 1985 on the advice of the police?

131. Which club signed a 44 year old TV presenter as reserve goalkeeper in November 1985?

132. Which two clubs were automatically promoted to the Premiership in 1996-97?

133. How many players were sent off in English League football on December 14 1985 to set a record?

134. In which club's ground did Middlesbrough have to play their first game of the 1986-87 season, when they were in the hands of the Official Receiver?

135. Which club were the first to be relegated from the First Division in 1996-97?

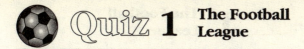

136. When did Ian Rush score his 200th goal for Liverpool?

137. Peter Shilton made his 1000th League appearance playing for which London club?

138. In which season were two substitutes allowed to be used for the first time in the Football League?

139. Which club lost 2-1 to Notts County in August 1986, their first League defeat in nine months, and first home defeat in a year?

140. Which two clubs contested a 6-6 draw in a Division Two match on October 22, 1960?

141. Up to the start of the 1997-98 season, only two clubs have completed a Football League season unbeaten. Name them.

142. Who called off their match against Bolton, in September 1987, following a dispute over how many police were needed at the match?

143. Who set a club record of 13 straight League wins in September 1987?

144. When West Ham beat Newcastle 8-1 in a Division One match in April 1986 which player scored against three different goalkeepers?

145. Which goalkeeper set a new record in 1995-96 by keeping 29 clean-sheets for Gillingham in the Third Division?

146. Who was the first, and so far only, club to play in the Premiership, all four previous divisions of the Football League and in both sections (North and South) of the old Third Division?

147. Which club had two points deducted for calling off their first match of the 1988-89 season because of building works on their ground?

148. Who became the first player to score 50 goals for a League club since 1960-61 when he scored 52 for Wolves in 1987-88?

149. From the start of which season were artificial pitches banned by the League?

150. Who was fined a week's wages for a sit down protest at half time in his side's opening match of the 1990 season?

136. 18 March 1987 137. Leyton Orient 138. 1987-8 139. Swindon Town 140. Charlton and Middlesbrough 141. Preston North End (1888-89) and Liverpool (1893-94) 142. Tranmere 143. Tottenham 144. Alvin Martin 145. Jim Stannard 146. Coventry City 147. Tottenham (points replaced with £15,000 fine) 148. Steve Bull 149. 119-92 150. Neville Southall

151. **Which club had their coach was wheel-clamped and towed away during a match at Chelsea in November 1990?**

152. Which club hold the record for the lowest Fourth Division attendance, only 625, for a game against Wrexham in December 1990?

153. **Who was the first club to win promotion on penalties, following their Fourth Division play-off?**

154. Millwall were successfully sued by three fans from which club because of a poor view they had at The New Den?

155. **Which club had four players sent off in their match against Northampton in September 1992?**

156. Which league decided to experiment with kick-ins instead of throw-ins in the 1994-95 season?

157. **Who was the first player to accumulate 61 disciplinary points in a League season?**

158. Who was the first player to score 30 goals in an English season in three consecutive years?

159. **Which club went through five managers in the 1995-96 season?**

160. Which club's first home ground was Plumstead Common?

161. **Whose record League win is 12-0 against Loughborough in 1900, and record League defeat is 0-8, also against Loughborough, four years earlier?**

162. Whose record League victory is 12-2 in a match against Accrington Stanley in 1892?

163. **Which club's highest League victory is 8-1, against Middlesbrough in the First Division in 1953?**

164. Which team set a club record when they beat Portsmouth 10-0 in Division One in 1928?

165. **Which club's record defeat is 1-9 by Birmingham in Division Two in 1959?**

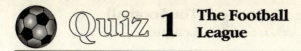
166. Who is currently Liverpool's highest scorer in one season, with 41 goals?

167. Which side won the first eleven games of their double winning season?

168. Whose record League victory is 10-1 against Huddersfield in November 1987?

169. Which club won their first ever League game 7-0 in 1892?

170. How many teams go into the play-offs every season?

171. Who did Middlesbrough beat 9-0 in 1958 to record their highest ever League victory?

172. Which 1997 Premiership club was originally called Stanley?

173. For which club does Wally Ardron hold the record for most League goals scored in a season, having scored 36 in 1950-51?

174. Who is the oldest League club in England?

175. What is the highest position that Oxford have ever finished in the top division?

176. Which club's record League attendance is 35,353 for their match against Leeds United in 1974?

177. Which club's record defeat is 1-16 against Southbank in the Northern League in 1919?

178. Which club played their first football league game on September 3 1892, when they won 1-0 away at Notts County?

179. Which club, who formerly played at the Antelope Ground, were runners-up in the 1983-84 First Division?

180. Who were the runners-up in the 1982-83 First Division championship?

181. **Which club lost 1-9 to Brighton and Hove Albion in 1965, their record defeat and Brighton's record win?**

182. Who were the four clubs who played in the 1996-97 First Division play-offs?

183. **Who beat Halifax 13-0 in 1934 to record their biggest League win?**

184. For which club is Harry Hardy the only player ever to have received an England cap?

185. **Which club played in Europe seven times but never played in the (old) First Division?**

186. Which team has a record league victory of 9-1 away at Newcastle and has spent every season bar one in the top two divisions?

187. **Which club established their record League win of 9-0 against Bristol Rovers in 1977?**

188. Who were the two clubs that produced the record score for a First Division match in 1948 at Maine Road?

189. **Who has made the most League appearances for Watford, with 415 games?**

190. Which club inflicted West Ham's worst defeat, 2-8 in 1963?

191. **Which club was known as Thames Ironworks FC when they were set up in 1895?**

192. Which player has made the most League appearances for West Ham?

193. **Against which team did Geoff Hurst score six goals in West Ham's record equalling 8-0 win in 1968?**

194. Which club's best ever placing in the League is fourth in the old third Division in the 1985-86 and 1986-87 seasons?

195. **Which club was formed in 1889, but only turned professional in 1964, and entered the League in 1978?**

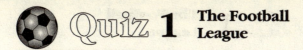

196. Who became the costliest player to leave Wimbledon in June 1995 and how what was the transfer fee?

197. Which club's record League victory was set at only 4-0 when they beat Scarborough in 1993?

198. When the Football League split into two divisions in 1892, which club first won the new Division One?

199. In what year did the Third Division North and the Third Division South combine to create one league?

200. After Liverpool, who won most (Old) First Division titles?

201. Which two clubs won the original Second Division the most, with six wins each?

202. In the 1988-89 season, Liverpool lost only one game after New Year's Day. Who beat the?

203. On which ground did Arsenal win the double in the 1970-71 season?

204. Who finished second when Tottenham won the League in 1961?

205. When was the last time that Tottenham were relegated?

206. Who was Tottenham's top goal scorer in 1979-80, with 19 goals?

207. Who beat Tottenham 6-0 at White Hart Lane in a League match in 1935?

208. Have Tottenham and Arsenal ever met in a League game outside the top division?

209. When was the first Arsenal/Tottenham League match?

210. Against which club did Argentinians Ossie Ardiles and Ricardo Villa make their Tottenham debut?

196. Warren Barton, £4m 197. **Wycombe Wanderers** 198. Sunderland 199. **1958** 200. Arsenal (10 times) **201. Leicester City and Manchester City** 202. Arsenal, in the last game of the season **203. White Hart Lane** 204. Sheffield Wednesday **205. 1976-77 season** 206. Glenn Hoddle 207. **Arsenal** 208. No **209. December 1909** 210. Nottingham Forest

Quiz 1

211. How long did it take Ricardo Villa to score his first League goal?

212. Who saved two penalties in a match against Liverpool in March 1973?

213. Who won Chelsea's Player of the Year award in 1976 and 1977?

214. Who is Chelsea's second highest scorer of League goals?

215. What is Chelsea's longest unbeaten run in a season?

216. What was the score when Manchester United beat West Ham to secure the 1966-67 title?

217. Who was Manchester United's leading scorer when they won the 1964-65 and 1966-67 titles?

218. Which club twice held Manchester United to draws durinh the Red Devils 1966-67 title winning season?

219. Only one club took maximum points at Old Trafford in Manchester United's 1966-67 title winning year. Name them.

220. Against which club did George Best score his first league goal?

221. Where did Manchester United win their only away game in the 1986-87 season?

222. Who scored the only hat-trick in Manchester United's 1985-86 season?

223. Against which club was Chelsea's record home attendance of 82,905 set in 1935?

224. Who has an average 0.78 goals per game for Chelsea, a club record?

225. Which team finished bottom of Division Three in 1996-97 to be relegated to the GM Vauxhall Conference?

211. 26 minutes 212. Tottenhma's Pat Jennings **213. Ray Wilkins** 214. Kerry Dixon **215. 27 matches** 216. 6-1 **217. Denis Law** 218. Liverpool **219. Leeds United** 220. Burnley **221. Anfield** 222. Jesper Olsen **223. Arsenal** 224. Jimmy Greaves **225. Hereford United**

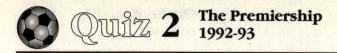

1. **Which Premiership favourites were beaten 4-2 by Norwich on the opening day of the season after leading 2-0?**

2. Which game was the first to be broadcast live on satellite television?

3. **Which two unfancied clubs had the only 100 per cent records after two games?**

4. A late goal against Southampton from which new signing gave Manchester United their first win of the season?

5. **Which Tottenham player was accused by the FA with feigning injury, the first case of its kind?**

6. Who scored a hat-trick for Leeds as they crushed Tottenham 5-0 in August?

7. **Which club's opening four defeats completed the worst start to the season in the manager's 17-year reign?**

8. Which team opened their £8m Centenary Stand in September?

9. **Which defender scored his first League goal for Liverpool in their 1-1 draw with Southampton in September?**

10. Which Manchester United striker broke his leg against Crystal Palace in September?

11. **Who was the Sheffield United goalkeeper sent off in their game against Spurs in September?**

12. Which Chelsea defender damaged knee ligaments in a clash with Dean Saunders in September, an injury which would eventually end his career?

13. **Whose late goal at Elland Road saved Leeds' long unbeaten home record?**

14. Which club were top of the League at the end of September?

15. **Against which club did Bryan Robson make his Premiership debut?**

16. Which player scored his 200th league goal in a 4-1 win over Middlesbrough in November?

17. **Whose hat-trick gave Norwich victory over Oldham and a place at the top of the Premiership in November?**

18. Which manager was banned from the touchline after three offences in three months?

19. **Which club ended Arsenal's run of six straight wins in November?**

20. How many points clear were Norwich in December?

21. **Which player was accused of throwing a punch at David Howells in December?**

22. Against which team did Liverpool suffer their worst defeat in 16 years in December?

23. **Norwich suffered their first home defeat in December against which team?**

24. Who hit his first QPR hat-trick in December against Everton?

25. **In which month did Manchester United hit the top of the Premiership for the first time?**

26. Which striker scored two hat-tricks in five days in January?

27. **Which club took over at the head of the Premiership with a 5-1 drubbing of Middlesbrough in January?**

28. Which club put a ban on players leaving while they are still in the running for silverware?

29. **Which player's penalty ended Liverpool's run of seven games without a win in January?**

30. Which player was sent off during Arsenal's 1-0 defeat at the hands of Liverpool in January?

16. Ian Rush 17. **Mark Robins** 18. Joe Kinnear 19. **Leeds** 20. Eight 21. **Ian Wright** 22. Coventry 23. **Ipswich** 24. Andy Sinton 25. **January** 26. Brian Deane 27. **Aston Villa** 28. Norwich City 29. **John Barnes** 30. Nigel Winterburn

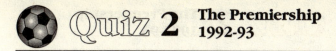

31. Which keeper was sent off for the second time in six weeks for handling outside his box in February?

32. Who were the reigning champions who were just outside the relegation zone in February?

33. Which player got a hostile reception when Manchester United travelled to Elland Road in February?

34. Which manager was sacked by Chelsea in February?

35. Which company signed a deal to sponsor the Premiership in February?

36. Who scored two goals in five minutes for Manchester United as they recovered from being 1-0 down against Southampton in February?

37. Whose hat-trick helped Tottenham to a 5-0 trouncing of Leeds in February?

38. Which team climbed off the bottom of the Premiership with victory over Middlesbrough in February?

39. Which makeshift striker scored for the seventh consecutive game for Sheffield Wednesday in February?

40. Which player was given a £20,000 fine in February for backing 'Soccer's Hard Men' video?

41. Whose late goal kept Aston Villa two points clear of Manchester United in February?

42. Which player was ruled out of an Arsenal game in February after needing 29 stitches from a fall down the stairs?

43. Which relegation-threatened side put six past Spurs in March, their worst defeat in 15 years?

44. For which Liverpool player did Aston Villa offer £3.5m in March?

45. Which club did Manchester United beat 2-1 in March to put them back top of the Premiership?

31. **Neville Southall** 32. Leeds United 33. **Eric Cantona** 34. Ian Porterfield 35. **Bass** 36. Ryan Giggs 37. **Teddy Sheringham** 38. Nottingham Forest 39. **Paul Warhurst** 40. Vinnie Jones 41. **Dwight Yorke** 42. Tony Adams 43. **Sheffield United** 44. John Barnes 45. Liverpool

46. Manchester United were rocked by defeat from which club, bottom of the Premiership, in March?

47. What was the score in the top-of-the-table clash between Manchester United and Aston Villa in March?

48. Which team halted Norwich's revival in March with a 3-0 win?

49. Which team went five points clear of the relegation zone with a win over Sheffield United in March?

50. Which manager was sent off in March for allegedly swearing at a linesman?

51. Which player was given the red card as he was being stretchered off after a clash with Viv Anderson in March?

52. Which QPR striker broke his leg twice in three months at the beginning of 1993?

53. Which Manchester United player was fined £1,000 in March for spitting at fans?

54. Which team did Oldham beat 6-2 in April to leap out of the relegation zone?

55. Which club were bottom of the Premiership at the start of April?

56. Which Forest defender was sent off at home to Blackburn in April?

57. Which team ended Norwich's title hopes in April with a 5-1 mauling?

58. On which away ground were Crystal Palace beaten 4-0 in April, compounding their relegation problems?

59. Two late headers from which player against Sheffield Wednesday put Manchester United back on the top of the Premiership in April?

60. Whose hat-trick for QPR in April kept Nottingham Forest at the bottom of the table?

61. **Who scored Manchester United's only goal against Ipswich in April to keep them top of the League?**

62. Who scored his first Aston Villa goal for a year when they beat Arsenal in April?

63. **Who scored a rare hat-trick for Sheffield Wednesday when they beat Southampton 5-2 on Easter Monday?**

64. Who scored a hat-trick for Norwich in April against Leeds to keep the embers of a title challenge alive?

65. **Which Coventry player's dismissal was revoked in April after referee Rodger Gilford watched the video?**

66. Which ex-Villa player scored his first hat-trick for Liverpool in their 4-0 win over Coventry in April?

67. **Which two rival clubs played out a 3-1 result which ended the title hopes of one team and helped the other out of relegation trouble in April?**

68. How many points clear were Manchester United with only two games left?

69. **Which Villa player was arrested for disorderly behaviour in April after an incident at an Essex nightclub?**

70. Brian Clough announced his retirement in April, after how many years in charge of Nottingham Forest?

71. **Against which team was Brian Clough's last home game in May?**

72. Which team were relegated with one remaining game, despite winning 3-2 at Hillsborough in their penultimate game?

73. **Which player was voted Footballer of the Year in May?**

74. Which team beat Villa 1-0 to give Manchester United the title?

75. **Manchester United's title put manager Alex Ferguson in the record books. Why?**

76. Who did Manchester United beat 3-1 to celebrate becoming champions?

77. How many Liverpool players were sent off during the season?

78. Who did Oldham beat 3-2 to keep alive their hopes of survival in May?

79. What was the score in the cup final rehearsal in May?

80. Who scored a hat-trick for Southampton in their 4-3 defeat at Oldham on the last day of the season?

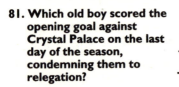

81. Which old boy scored the opening goal against Crystal Palace on the last day of the season, condemning them to relegation?

82. Against which team did Norwich draw 3-3 to give them third place on the last day of the season?

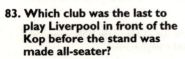

83. Which club was the last to play Liverpool in front of the Kop before the stand was made all-seater?

84. Which player scored his 300th goal for his club on the last day of the season?

85. Which team finished the season without an away win?

86. What is the final gap at the top of the Premiership between Manchester United and Aston Villa?

87. Which player was attacked by the crowd on the final day of the season when Manchester United played Wimbledon?

88. Who was the leading scorer for the season?

89. Which player was Blackburn's leading scorer for the season?

90. In which position did Liverpool end a season in which they were criticised for their tactics?

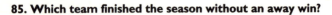

1. **Which goalkeeper scored in the 1967 Charity Shield?**

2. Which goalkeeper was beaten by Jennings' huge kick?

3. **Which teams were involved in that game and how did it finish?**

4. What is the highest number of goals scored in a season's competition?

5. **When was it?**

6. When was the first Charity Shield match played at Wembley?

7. **Which teams were involved?**

8. In 1974, two players were sent-off in the Charity Shield. Who were they?

9. **What was so special about that moment?**

10. Who won that ill-tempered match?

11. **When was the first ever Charity Shield?**

12. What was the result?

13. **No Charity Shield has ever finished goalless. True or false?**

14. Why was the 1950 Charity Shield completely different from the other years?

15. **Which club has appeared in the most consecutive Charity Shield's?**

1. **Pat Jennings** 2. Alex Stepney 3. **Tottenham and Manchester United. The score was 3-3.** 4. 12 5. **In 1911, when Manchester United beat Swindon Town 8-4** 6. 1974 7. **Liverpool and Leeds** 8. Kevin Keegan and Billy Bremner 9. **It was the first time that a sending-off had occured in the competition** 10. Liverpool - on penalties 11. **1908** 12. Manchester United beat QPR 4-0 in a replay after a 1-1 draw 13. **False - Liverpool and Manchester United drew 0-0 in 1977** 14. A World Cup XI met the Canadian Touring Team 15. **Everton**

16. What was their record?

17. Which team has won most Charity Shield matches?

18. Who scored a hat-trick for Leeds United in the 1992 Charity Shield?

19. Who scored the only goal in the 1995 Charity Shield between Everton and Blackburn?

20. How many Charity Shield contests have been settled by a penalty shoot-out?

21. How many times has the Charity Shield been shared?

22. When was the last year it was shared?

23. Who was involved?

24. Who scored an overhead kick for Manchester United in the 1994 Charity Shield?

25. When was the first time the trophy was shared?

26. Who were the two teams?

27. What was so different about the Charity Shield matches in 1913 and from 1923 to 1926?

28. Derby County have never won the Charity Shield. True or false?

29. Who were the first London club to win the Charity Shield?

30. What has been the biggest winning margin in Charity Shield's?

16. Four - between 1984 and 1987 17. **Manchester United** 18. Eric Cantona 19.
Vinny Samways 20. Two - in 1974 and 1993 21. **Eleven** 22. 1991 23. **Arsenal
and Tottenham** 24. Paul Ince 25. 1949 26. Portsmouth and Wolves 27. **A team
of amateurs played professionals each year.** 28. False - they won it in 1975 29.
Tottenham - in 1921 30. Five goals - in 1913, 1925, 1968 and 1978

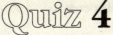
1. **Which referee was in charge for the 1966 FA Cup final and the 1974 World Cup Final?**

2. Who refereed the 1996 FA Cup final?

3. **Who was the referee for the 1997 Chelsea vs Leicester FA Cup quarter final, decided by a controversial penalty decision?**

4. Who was the referee that sent off five players in the Chesterfield/Plymouth match in the 1996-97 season?

5. **How many Premier League referees were there in the 1996-97 season?**

6. How many 1996-97 English referees are on the FIFA list?

7. **How many referees are on the National List, used in all four English Divisions?**

8. Who was the referee for the 1995 FA Cup final?

9. **Who was in charge for the 1990 World Cup final?**

10. Which referee sent off Kevin Moran in the 1985 FA Cup final?

11. **What was the monstrous name of the Austrian referee that was in charge for two World Cup qualifiers in 1934 and 1937?**

12. Who was England's only referee in the 1990 World Cup Finals?

13. **Which English referee was in charge for the Third Place Play-Off in Mexico 86?**

14. Who was the Northern Irish referee in the 1986 and 1990 World Cups?

15. **Who was the Scottish referee in the 1982 World Cup Finals?**

1. **Jack Taylor** 2. Dermot Gallacher 3. **Mike Reed** 4. Andrew D'Urso 5. 19 6. 8 7. 69 8. Gerald Ashby 9. **Mr Codesal (Mexico)** 10. Peter Willis 11. **Herr Frankenstein** 12. George Courtney 13. **George Courtney** 14. Mr Snoddy 15. **Mr Valentine**

16. Who was the English referee at the 1982 World Cup Finals?

17. **Who was the referee that refused to allow Brazil's injury time winner in their 1978 World Cup match against Sweden?**

18. Who refereed the 1994 World Cup Final?

19. **Who was the English referee that was in charge for the Third Place Play Play Off in the 1966 World Cup Finals?**

20. Which World Cup Final did England's Mr Ling referee?

21. **Who was the referee for the 1994 FA Cup final?**

22. Who refereed the 1995-96 League Cup final?

23. **Who was the high profile referee that retired after his match at Crystal Palace in April 1995?**

24. Who was the referee for England's semi-final in Euro 96?

25. **Who was the Scottish referee for the France/Czech Republic semi-final in Euro 96?**

26. Who refereed the Euro 96 final?

27. **What nationality was the referee for England's 4-1 win over Holland in Euro 96?**

28. Who refereed the 1994-95 Coca Cola Cup final?

29. **Who refereed the 1995 Chairty Shield when Everton beat Blackburn1-0?**

30. How much does a referee earn for a 1996-97 Premiership match?

1. **Who scored a hat-trick on the opening day of the season in the game between Arsenal and Coventry?**

2. Who scored a rare brace when Liverpool met Sheffield Wednesday on the opening day of the season?

3. **Which two future teammates scored when Manchester United drew 1-1 with Newcastle United in August?**

4. Who scored a hat-trick for Everton in August as they beat Sheffield United 4-2?

5. **Which club brought to an end Liverpool's run of four wins at the start of the season?**

6. Against which club did Swindon win their first point of the season?

7. **Who sat at the top of the Premiership after five games?**

8. Which £750,000 signing from Oldham scored four goals in his first five games at his new club?

9. **Which new signing scored a brace for Manchester United when they beat Sheffield United in August?**

10. How many goals did Swindon concede in their first four matches?

11. **Who scored Sheffield Wednesday's first goal of the season, in their fifth game?**

12. Who was sent off for the first time in his career when Coventry beat Liverpool in September?

13. **Who hit a hat-trick for Arsenal when they beat Ipswich 4-0 in September?**

14. Which two players scored three goals in two minutes for Tottenham when they beat Oldham 5-0 in September?

15. **Which two Liverpool players had a heated argument during their derby game with Everton in September?**

1. Mick Quinn 2. Nigel Clough **3. Ryan Giggs and Andy Cole** 4. Tony Cottee **5. Tottenham Hotspur** 6. Norwich **7. Manchester United** 8. Ian Marshall **9. Roy Keane** 10. 14 **11. Mark Bright** 12. Rob Jones **13. Kevin Campbell** 14. Teddy Sheringham and Steve Sedgeley **15. Bruce Grobelaar and Steve McManaman**

16. Whose goal decided the top-of-the-table clash between Liverpool and Arsenal in September?

17. Which striker, who would later gain fame at a London club, scored four goals for Norwich at Everton in September?

18. Which Dutchman was sent off within 24 minutes of his West Ham debut in September?

19. Who scored the first of many goals for Liverpool in their 2-1 victory over Oldham in October?

20. Just 3,039 turned up to watch Wimbledon on Boxing Day in 1993. Who were they playing?

21. Which Leeds striker finished with 17 goals in 1993-94?

22. Which striker went missing when he complained he was homesick for his friends and family in London?

23. Which team had scored just once in six Premiership games going into November?

24. Which club recorded six successive League defeats, their worst run since 1941, to leave them in the bottom three in November?

25. Which two internationals scored braces in the Manchester derby in November?

26. Which Ipswich player celebrated his 600th appearance for the club in a 2-2 draw with Swindon in November?

27. Which Hammer scored in their 2-0 win over Oldham in November at the grand old age of 35?

28. Who scored his first Premiership hat-trick for QPR in their win at Goodison Park in November?

29. Which striker made it 15 goals in 16 League games when he hit a hat-trick against Liverpool in November?

30. Which team did Swindon beat for thier first win of the season in November?

16. Eric Cantona **17. Efan Ekoku** 18. Jeroen Boere **19. Robbie Fowler** 20. Everton **21. Rod Wallace** 22. Andy Cole **23. Arsenal** 24. Chelsea **25. Niall Quinn and Eric Cantona** 26. John Walk **27. Alvin Martin** 28. Bradley Allen **29. Andy Cole** 30. QPR

31. **Which player clashed with John Fashanu and fractured his cheekbone in November?**

32. Who did David Seaman foul to receive the red card when Arsenal met West Ham in November?

33. **Which Leeds striker scored his fourth goal in five games when they beat Manchester City 3-2 in December?**

34. Which team did Coventry beat in December for Phil Neal's first victory as manager?

35. **What was the score in the North London derby at Highbury in December?**

36. By how many points were Manchester United leading on December 7?

37. **Who scored a well-taken own goal to salvage a point for Sheffield Wednesday at Aston Villa in December?**

38. Which two QPR players were sent off when they were beaten 3-2 by Liverpool in December?

39. **Which Liverpool defender scored four minutes from the whistle to save them from a home defeat against lowly Swindon in December?**

40. How many years separate the birthdates of Robbie Fowler and Mickey Hazard, two scorers in the Tottenham v Liverpool game in December?

41. **Who scored the own goal which started Sheffield Wednesday's five-goal rout over West Ham in December?**

42. Which club was only one point ahead of bottom-placed Swindon in December?

43. **Who scored a hat-trick for Arsenal in their 4-0 win at Swindon in December?**

44. Who scored for Liverpool against Wimbledon in December, a year before joining the Reds?

45. **Who scored a rare brace for Swindon as they recorded a 3-3 draw at Sheffield Wednesday?**

31. Gary Mabbutt 32. Trevor Morley **33. Brian Deane** 34. Arsenal **35.** 1-1 36. 15 **37. Shaun Teale** 38. Simon Barker and Les Ferdinand **39. Mark Wright** 40. 15 **41. Mike Marsh** 42. Chelsea **43. Kevin Campbell** 44. John Scales **45. Craig Maskell**

46. Which Southampton player was sent off for elbowing Norwich's Ruel Fox on New Year's Day?

47. Who were Manchester City leading 2-0 when play was abandoned on New Year's Day?

48. Which Chelsea player scored his first senior goal when they beat Everton 4-2 on New Years' Day?

49. Who scored a brace for Liverpool when they clawed their way back from 3-0 down against Manchester United in January?

50. Which Owl scored his 12th goal of the season to silence Tottenham in January?

51. Who scored a hat-trick for Everton when they recorded a rare victory, a 6-2 win over Swindon in January?

52. With which team did Wimbledon have a on-pitch brawl with in January?

53. Who was stunned by a 2-1 defeat at Swindon in January?

54. In January a minute's silence was observed at all grounds after the death of which legendary figure?

55. Which two players had both scored 23 Premiership goals by January 23?

56. Who headed home the equaliser for West Ham against Norwich in January, only seconds after coming on as a substitute?

57. Which much-touted striker scored his only goal for Everton in a 4-2 victory over Chelsea in February?

58. Who hit a hat-trick for Swindon when they beat Coventry in February?

59. When Villa put five past Swindon in February, who netted a hat-trick?

60. Who was Newcastle captain for the day when they were beaten 4-2 by Wimbledon at Selhurst Park?

46. Francis Benali 47. **Ipswich** 48. Craig Burley 49. **Nigel Clough** 50. Mark Bright 51. **Tony Cottee** 52. Sheffield Wednesday 53. **Tottenham Hotspur** 54. Matt Busby 55. **Alan Shearer and Andy Cole** 56. Trevor Morley 57. **Brett Angell** 58. Jan-Aage Fjortoft 59. **Dean Saunders** 60. Peter Beardsley

61. Southampton's hat-trick man when they beat Liverpool 4-2 in February was which international?

62. Which Blackburn defender scored their only goal when they triumphed over Newcastle in February?

63. Who scored Norwich's late equaliser to deny Swindon their fifth win of the season in February?

64. Who did John Polston wrestle to the ground to receive his red card when Norwich drew with Blackburn in February?

65. Who returned from injury to complete a hat-trick as Newcastle met Coventry in February?

66. Whose goal gave Arsenal their first victory in six League games when they played Blackburn in February?

67. Which Swindon player ensured that his team were rooted to the bottom when he scored an own goal in their game at Maine Road in February?

68. Which Spurs defender brought down Gavin Peacock to give Chelsea a last-minute penalty and equaliser in February?

69. Who saved two penalties when Aston Villa and Spurs met in February?

70. Manchester United's first home defeat in 17 months was inflicted by which team?

71. Whose injury-time equaliser salvaged a point for Tottenham when they played Sheffield United in February?

72. How many goals did Newcastle score when they faced bottom-placed Swindon in February?

73. Who was second in the Premiership at the start of March?

74. Who missed two months of action with a broken leg but returned to score in the Merseyside derby in March?

75. Which Chelsea player scored for both teams when they met Liverpool in March?

61. Matthew Le Tissier 62. David May 63. Jeremy Goss 64. Alan Shearer 65. Andy Cole 66. Paul Merson 67. Kevin Horlock 68. Dean Austin 69. Mark Bosnich 70. Chelsea 71. Jason Dozzell 72. Seven 73. Blackburn 74. Robbie Fowler 75. Craig Burley

76. Which two players were on the scoresheet when Arsenal beat Southampton 4-0 at the Dell in March?

77. Which Manchester United player scored an own goal when they travelled to Highbury in March?

78. Which father and son met when Everton played Tottenham in March?

79. Who beat Southampton in March to climb out of the relegation spot and leave the Saints in their place?

80. Who scored a goal on his debut for Manchester City, after being signed two minutes before the transfer deadline?

81. Which Norwegian international scored a brace at Anfield to give Sheffield United hope of avoiding relegation?

82. Who scored the goals in Blackburn's top-of-the-table clash with Manchester United in April?

83. Which two McCarthys scored for Oldham when they beat QPR in March?

84. How many goals were scored when Norwich met Southampton in April?

85. Who beat Blackburn to prevent them going top of the table in April?

86. Whose late equaliser for QPR left Blackburn two points behind Manchester United with two games to play?

87. Who scored two goals for Sheffield United as they beat Newcastle in April, climbing out of the relegation zone?

88. Who beat Blackburn to end their last hopes of winning the Premiership?

89. Who scored the goal which ensured Everton's survival in the last game of the season?

90. Who beat Sheffield United to condemn them to relegation in their last game of the season?

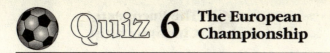

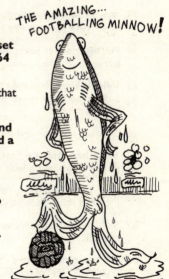

1. In which year was the first final held?

2. The USSR were awarded a walkover into the semi-finals in the 1960 championships. Why?

3. **Which stadium hosted the first final, attracting only 17,966 spectators?**

4. How many teams entered the first championships?

5. **Which Dane was the top scorer in the 1964 Championship with 11 goals?**

6. Which was the first tournament entered by England?

7. **Why did Greece refuse to play Albania in 1964, giving the Albanians a walkover into the second round?**

8. In which city did England play their first European game v France?

9. **The home leg v France in 1962 was which English manager's last game in charge?**

10. Which manager took over the reins for the second leg, which England lost 5-2?

THE AMAZING... FOOTBALLING MINNOW!

11. **Which team did Northern Ireland upset to go into the second round of the 1964 competition?**

12. Which future N.Ireland manager scored in that game?

13. **Which legendary Soviet goalkeeper and European Footballer of the Year saved a penalty to help them beat Italy in the 1964 championships?**

14. Which footballing minnow put Holland out of the 1964 competition, despite electing to play both legs in Holland?

15. **Which Swede played his 80th international in the second round tie they eventually lost to the Soviets?**

16. A crowd of over 100,000 saw Spain beat which country in the 1964 final?

17. **Which legendary Italian topped the scoring charts for the 1968 championships?**

18. Which player scored the winning goal for Republic of Ireland v Czechoslovakia in the 1968 qualifying competition, only days after breaking through to the Fulham first team?

19. **Which future Wimbledon manager played in that campaign for the Republic of Ireland?**

20. Which team did West Germany meet in the game billed as the 'Match of the Year' in the 1968 qualifying competition?

21. **Which country held West Germany to a 0-0 draw in 1968 to ensure that the World Cup finalists did not qualify for the European quarter-finals?**

22. Which Celtic veteran made his international debut at the age of 36 at Wembley v England in Scotland's qualifying game for the 1968 championship?

23. **Which Northern Ireland player put paid to Scotland's hopes of qualifying for the 1968 tournament?**

24. The biggest-ever European Championship crowd of 134,000 were attracted to which venue?

25. **Which English player limped off with a broken toe v Scotland, but came back on to score in the qualifying for the 1968 tournament?**

26. By which unusual method did Italy progress to the 1968 final?

27. **Who became the first English player to be sent off in an international when he was red-carded in the 1968 semi-final?**

28. Who were England's two scorers when they beat the Soviet Union in the 1968 third-place play-off?

29. **Which team won the 1968 championships in front of a home crowd?**

30. Which German topped the 1972 scoring charts with 11, and was the undoubted star of the tournament?

29. Italy 30. Gerd Muller

16. Soviet Union 17. **Luigi Riva** 18. Turloch O'Connor 19. **Joe Kinnear** 20. Czechoslovakia 21. **Albania** 22. Ronnie Simpson 23. **George Best** 24. Hampden Park (Scotland v England in 1968) 25. **Jackie Charlton** 26. They beat the Soviet Union on the toss of a coin 27. **Alan Mullery** 28. Bobby Charlton and Geoff Hurst

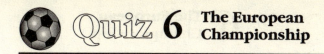
31. Which country's World Cup squad was hit by a series of bans for alleged 'commercial activities', leaving them with a decimated 1972 European Championship team?

32. Who scored England's equaliser at Wembley v Switzerland to help them into the 1972 finals?

33. Which British team lost all their away games and won all their home games while trying to qualify for the 1972 finals?

34. Who was the goalkeeper who helped West Germany scrape into the 1972 quarter-finals after only drawing in Turkey?

35. Who scored the only English goal in their 1972 quarter-final defeat by West Germany?

36. Which country hosted the final stages of the 1972 tournament?

37. Who reached their third final in four attempts in 1972, losing to West Germany?

38. Which Irish player topped the scoring charts for the 1976 European Championships, although his country failed to qualify for the quarter-finals?

39. Which manager was in charge of England's campaign to qualify for the 1976 finals?

40. Who scored all five goals when England beat Cyprus at Wembley while trying to qualify for the 1976 European Championships?

41. Which England player scored against Czechoslovakia in a game which ended 2-1 and effectively ended their chances of qualifying for the 1976 competition?

42. Who were the only team to beat Wales in their qualification for the 1976 quarter-finals?

43. Who was the Welsh manager who led them to their first European quarter-final?

44. Which 34-year-old Wrexham player was the Welsh hero when he scored the winner against Austria to ensure their qualification for the 1976 quarter-finals?

45. Who was the Scottish keeper for the 1976 campaign, which ended at the group stages?

46. Who was Ireland's player-manager for their 1976 campaign, which also ended at the group stages?

47. **When the Republic of Ireland travelled to Russia in 1975 which club side was playing as the Soviet national team?**

48. Which team embarrassed East Germany with a 2-1 win, winning their first game in the history of the competition in the group stages of the 1976 competition?

49. **The quarter-final between Wales and Yugoslavia in 1976 was almost abandoned. Why?**

50. The 1976 final was the first to be decided by penalties. Who were the two teams involved?

51. **Who was the only player to miss in the 1976 penalty shoot-out?**

52. Which English player top-scored in the 1980 campaign with seven goals?

53. **Which country was chosen to host the 1980 finals?**

54. What was the final result in the first-ever meeting between the Republic and Northern Ireland in the qualifying for the 1980 championships?

55. **Who were the only team to take a point from England in the 1980 qualifying stage?**

56. Which England player was substituted in their game v Bulgaria in 1979 after scoring and then clashing with Grancharov?

57. **Who scored from the penalty spot to give Scotland a win over Norway in the 1980 qualifying tournament?**

58. Who scored Scotland's only goal when they were trounced 3-1 by Belgium in the 1980 group stages?

59. **Which country was the surprise package of the 1980 qualifying tournament, reaching the finals despite failing to win away from home?**

60. Which Welsh player was sent off against Turkey in 1979 after breaking the cheekbone of Mustapha I, who was duly taken off to be replaced by Mustapha II?

46. Johnny Giles **47. Dynamo Kiev 48.** Iceland **49. The Yugoslav keeper Maric was hit by a beer can thrown by a Welsh fan 50.** Czechoslavakia and West Germany **51. Uli Hoeness 52.** Kevin Keegan **53.** Italy **54.** 0-0 **55. Republic of Ireland 56.** Peter Barnes **57. Archie Gemmill 58.** John Robertson **59. Greece 60.** Byron Stevenson

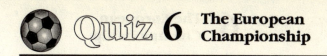

61. **Who was the unlikely hat-trick hero when West Germany beat Holland in the 1980 finals?**

62. Who were England's opponents in the 1980 finals when the Italian police used tear gas to disperse rioting fans?

63. **Who had a 'goal' disallowed in that 1-1 draw?**

64. Who scored the only goal for Italy in their victory over England in the 1980 tournament?

65. **Whose ineffective tackle allowed Graziani to cross for the goal?**

66. Who scored a brace in the 1980 final to give West Germany victory?

67. **Who were their opponents?**

68. Which French genius was the star of the 1984 tournament and finished as top scorer?

69. **Which country hosted the 1984 finals?**

70. Which West Ham player scored for Belgium in their 1983 qualifying game against East Germany?

71. **Who scored Scotland's two goals when they beat East Germany for their only victory of the group stages for the 1984 tournament?**

72. Who scored England's two goals in the opening game of their 1984 qualifying campaign against Denmark?

73. **Who scored the last-minute equaliser for Denmark to make the score 2-2?**

74. Which team did England beat 3-0 for Bobby Robson's first victory as manager?

75. **Who scored a hat-trick in his first appearance on the England starting line-up when they beat Luxembourg 9-0 at Wembley in 1983?**

76. Who handled the ball in England's crunch tie with Denmark at Wembley in Dec 1983, giving away a penalty?

77. **Who stepped up to score the penalty and put an end to England's hopes of qualifying?**

78. Wales could have qualified for the 1984 finals had they beaten Yugoslavia in Cardiff. Who scored the Welsh goal in the 1-1 draw?

79. **Which Northern Ireland player scored the only goal in their historic home victory over West Germany in 1982?**

80. Which Northern Ireland player won his 100th cap against Austria in a European Championship game in 1983?

81. **Which Manchester United player scored his first international goal in the same game?**

82. Which team qualified for the 1984 finals with a 12-1 win over Malta, prompting claims of match-fixing as they had to win by 11 clear goals?

83. **Which team failed to qualify for the finals because of that freak result?**

84. Which future Charlton Athletic player broke his leg in the opening game of the 1984 finals?

85. **Which French defender headbutted Jesper Olsen, getting himself sent off and suspended for the next three games?**

86. Which 18-year-old Belgian orchestrated their victory over Yugoslavia in the 1984 finals?

87. **Platini scored two hat-tricks in the 1984 finals. Which teams were on the receiving end of his stunning displays?**

88. Which veteran Portuguese striker scored on his record 65th international appearance v Romania, taking them through to the 1984 semi-finals?

89. **Whose 119th-minute cross set up Platini for the semi-final winner over Portugal in 1984?**

90. Who was the Spanish goalkeeper and captain who dropped the ball over the line from a Platini free-kick in the final?

76. Phil Neal 77. **Allan Simonsen** 78. Robbie James 79. **Norman Whiteside** 80. Pat Jennings 81. **Norman Whiteside** 82. Spain 83. **Holland** 84. Allan Simonsen 85. **Luis Arconada**
Manuel Amoros 86. Enzo Scifo 87. **Belgium and Yugoslavia** 88. Nene 89.
Jean Tigana 90. Luis Arconada

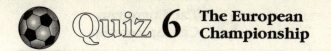

91. Which country was selected as the venue for the 1988 finals?

92. Who were the only team to take a point from England in their qualification for the 1988 finals?

93. How many goals did Gary Lineker score in England's six qualifying games?

94. How many goals did England put past Turkey at Wembley in 1987?

95. Which two players scored the only goals of Northern Ireland's unsuccessful qualifying campaign for the 1988 finals?

96. The 8-0 victory by Holland over Cyprus in the 1988 qualifying competition was declared void. Why?

97. Which Welsh player was refused permission to play against Denmark in the 1988 qualifying by his Italian bosses?

98. Who scored the winning goal for Wales in that game in Cardiff?

99. Which veteran Republic of Ireland defender was controversially picked for their 1988 qualifying game v Scotland and silenced the critics with a winning goal?

100. Which Scottish player ensured the Republic of Ireland's qualification for the 1988 finals when his late goal took both points against Bulgaria?

101. Which English referee took control of the opening match of the 1988 finals when Italy drew with West Germany?

102. Which Italian scored his first international goal in that game?

103. Who was the Italian goalkeeper whose extra steps were penalised, leading to the West German equaliser?

104. Which Spaniard's clearly offside goal helped them to victory over Denmark in their first match of the 1988 finals?

105. Which future Premiership stars scored for West Germany and Italy respectively in that 1988 tournament?

106. Which German scored his first and second international goals in their win over Spain in the 1988 finals?

107. Who was the Danish goalkeeper who had a nightmare game against Italy in 1988, gifting them a 2-0 victory when they only required a draw to qualify for the semi-finals?

108. Who was the manager of West Germany in 1988?

109. Whose goal gave the Republic of Ireland victory over England in their clash in the 1988 finals?

110. Who was the England keeper beaten by that goal?

111. That game almost turned around because of a timely England substitution. Who replaced Neil Webb?

112. When Holland and England met in the 1988 finals, which Dutch striker scored a hat-trick to end England's semi-final hopes?

113. Which player scored the only England goal in that game?

114. Who was Ireland's manager who almost took them into the 1988 semi-finals?

115. Whose superb volley gave the Republic the lead in their game v the Soviet Union in 1988?

116. What was the result in the game between the Soviet Union and England which sealed England's nightmare 1988 tournament?

117. Ireland needed only a draw against Holland to reach the semi-finals. Which Dutch player came on as a substitute to score a late goal and spoil the party?

118. Who presented Peter Shilton with a bouquet of flowers for his 100th cap in the 1988 finals?

119. Holland met West Germany in the 1988 semi-finals. When was the last time that Holland had beaten the Germans?

120. Which German player suffered stomach pains in the warm-up to that Holland semi-final and so had to be replaced for that game?

106. Rudi Voller **107. Peter Schmeichel** 108. Franz Beckenbauer **109. Ray Houghton** 110. Peter Shilton **111. Glenn Hoddle** 112. Marco Van Basten **113. Bryan Robson** 114. Jackie Charlton **115. Ronnie Whelan** 116. 3-1 **117. Wim Kieft** 118. Ruud Gullit **119. 1956** 120. Pierre Littbarski

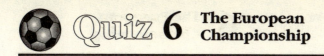
121. Who tripped Klinsmann to give West Germany a penalty in their semi-final?

122. Who stepped up to score the semi-final penalty for West Germany in the 1988 finals?

123. Which German player tripped Marco Van Basten to give Holland a penalty?

124. Who was the German keeper, later to play in the Premiership, who was beaten by Ronald Koeman's penalty?

125. Whose pass set up Van Basten for his winner against West Germany in the 1988 semi-finals?

126. How many Soviet players had been booked going into their semi-final clash with Italy in 1988?

127. Who scored the Soviet Union's second goal to send them into the 1988 final?

128. Who scored the first Dutch goal in the 1988 finals between Holland and the Soviet Union?

129. Whose cross set up Van Basten for the 1988 final's second goal?

130. In which city was the 1988 final held?

131. Who was the manager of the winning Dutch team?

132. Which Danish player featured in the 1988 tournament at the age of 38?

133. Which French striker finished the 1992 tournament as the top scorer in the campaign with 11 goals?

134. Which country was selected as hosts for the 1992 finals?

135. Which team were delayed en route to their qualifying game in Reykjavik in 1990, held at Heathrow for alleged shoplifting offences?

121. **Frank Rijkaard** 122. Lothar Matthaus 123. **Jurgen Kohler** 124. Eike Immel 125. **Jan Wouters** 126. Seven 127. **Oleg Protasov** 128. Ruud Gullit 129. **Arnold Muhren** 130. Munich 131. **Rinus Michels** 132. Morten Olsen 133. **Jean-Pierre Papin** 134. Sweden 135. **Albania**

136. Which ex-Nottingham Forest player helped Iceland to a historic qualifying win over Spain?

137. Which Scottish player scored the winner against Romania at Hampden Park to begin their successful qualifying campaign for the 1992 tournament?

138. What was the score when Scotland met Bulgaria in Sofia while trying to qualify for the 1992 championships?

139. Which player was penalised for handling the ball in his own area when the Scots travelled to Romania for their qualifier?

140. How many goals did Scotland score in their two ties with San Marino in the 1992 qualification campaign?

141. Which team qualified for the 1992 tournament ahead of Italy?

142. Which country did the Faroe Islands beat in their first ever European Championship game?

143. Brian Laudrup pulled out of the Danish international team after disagreements with their manager. Who was he?

144. The Danes finished second in their qualifying group but made it to the finals. Why?

145. What score was Northern Ireland's home fixture against the Faroe Islands?

146. Who scored his first international goal for two years when Wales met Belgium at Cardiff Arms Park for their qualifier in 1990?

147. Which Welsh player was sent off against Luxembourg in the same qualifying series?

148. Who was the scorer when Wales pulled off a magnificent victory over Germany in 1991?

149. Who were the only team to take a point from Holland in their qualification for the 1992 championships?

150. Who was the England manager when they began their campaign to qualify for the 1992 tournament?

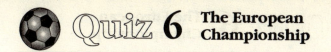

151. Who scored an Irish hat-trick when they demolished Turkey in 1990?

152. Which controversial figure was dropped for England's visit to the Republic of Ireland in their qualifying game?

153. Who scored the two goals when England met the Republic at Wembley?

154. Whose scrambled goal gave England the points in Turkey to leave them favourites to qualify for 1992?

155. Who scored the goal 13 minutes from the final whistle to earn England a draw against Poland and seal their qualification for the 1992 finals?

156. Who was the French goalkeeper who kept them in the opening game of the 1992 finals against Sweden?

157. Which English player was drafted in at right-back against Denmark because of injuries?

158. Who replaced him late in the game and twice came close to scoring?

159. Which Danish player, later to play in England, beat Chris Woods but hit the post in that game?

160. Which French player headbutted Stuart Pearce in their 1992 Championship game?

161. Which English player cleared off the line from an Angloma header in the France v England clash in 1992?

162. Which Swedish player scored their only goal as they beat Denmark in the group stages of the 1992 championships?

163. Who scored England's only goal of the 1992 finals?

164. Who chipped the deciding penalty in the shoot-out to win the 1976 finals for Czechoslovakia?

165. Who replaced Gary Lineker when Graham Taylor substituted him in their final 1992 game against Sweden?

Quiz 6 The European Championship

166. In which minute did Brolin score the winner in that game?

167. Who scored the winner for Denmark against France, sealing their move into the 1992 semi-finals?

168. Which future Premiership star scored the only goal when Holland met Scotland in the group stages of the 1992 finals?

169. Which German played on until half-time against the CIS despite suffering a broken arm after 20 minutes in 1992?

170. Whose last-minute 'fall' earned Germany a free-kick and the equaliser against the CIS in the 1992 finals?

171. Who scored the free-kick for Germany to draw their game with the CIS in 1992?

172. Who was the Scotland manager who guided them in the 1992 finals?

173. Who scored Germany's first goal in their 2-0 win over Scotland in 1992?

174. Which Scottish defender deflected Stefan Effenberg's cross into his own net for the second German goal in 1992?

175. Which German player came on as a substitute against Scotland in 1992 but went off five minutes later after clashing heads with Stuart McCall?

176. Which future Premiership keeper played in the 1992 finals for the CIS?

177. What was the score in the 1992 clash between Holland and Germany?

178. Who scored his first international goal in Scotland's 3-0 win over the CIS in 1992?

179. Who was brought down for a penalty in Scotland's 3-0 victory over the CIS in 1992?

180. Who was Germany's keeper in their semi-final tie with Sweden in 1992?

166. 82nd **167. Johnny Elstrup** 168. Dennis Bergkamp **169. Rudi Völler** 170. Jürgen Klinsmann **171. Thomas Hässler** 172. Andy Roxburgh **173. Karl Heinz Riedle** 174. Maurice Malpas **175. Stefan Reuter** 176. Dmitri Kharine **177. 3-1** 178. Brian McClair **179. Pat Nevin** 180. Bodo Illgner

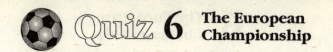
181. **Which lofty striker scored Sweden's final goal of the 1992 championships?**

182. Who scored a brace for Germany in their semi-final clash with Sweden in 1992?

183. **Who scored a brace for Denmark in their semi-final game against Holland in 1992?**

184. Which Danish player suffered an horrific knee injury in their clash with Holland in the 1992 semi-finals?

185. **Who scored Holland's 85th-minute equaliser in their semi-final with Denmark in 1992?**

186. In the penalty shoot-out to decide the semi-final between Holland and Denmark in 1992, who was the only man to miss?

187. **In which city was the final of the 1992 championships held?**

188. Which future Premiership player scored in the 1992 final between Denmark and Germany?

189. **Which was the only team not to play a qualifying game for the 1996 Championship?**

190. Which two Premiership players scored in Romania's win over Azerbaijan in the qualifying tournament for Euro 96?

191. **Which three countries reached the finals for the first time in 1996?**

192. Which player topped the scoring charts for the European qualifying rounds with 12 goals?

193. **Who were the only nation to beat Italy in their qualification for the 1996 Championship?**

194. In which English city did Holland play the Republic of Ireland for the final place in Euro 96?

195. **Who scored the winner when Northern Ireland beat Austria in Vienna in the qualification stages of Euro 96?**

Liverpool 195. Phil Gray
Turkey, Switzerland and Croatia 192. Davor Suker 193. Croatia 194.
188. John Jensen 189. England 190. Dan Petrescu and Florin Raducioiu 191.
Henrik Andersen 185. Frank Rijkaard 186. Marco Van Basten 187. Gothenberg
181. Kennet Andersson 182. Karl Heinz Riedle 183. Henrik Larsen 184.

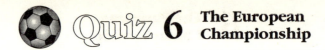
196. Who scored for the Welsh in Dusseldorf when thay pulled off a draw against Germany in their unsuccessful qualifying campaign for Euro 96?

197. Which two players topped the Scottish scoring charts in their qualifying campaign for Euro 96?

198. Who scored the opening goal of Euro 96?

199. Which Swiss player equalised with a penalty against England in 1996?

200. Who provided the pass for England's opening goal of Euro 96?

201. Who captained the England team for their first game of Euro 96?

202. Which three Glasgow Rangers' players scored goals in the 1996 championships?

203. At which ground did Scotland eke out a draw with Holland in the 1996 tournament?

204. Holland appealed for a penalty in their Euro 96 tie with Scotland, claiming handball. Which player was accused?

205. Which player was judged to have fouled Gordon Durie to earn Scotland their penalty against England in 1996?

206. Whose penalty did David Seaman save in the 1996 clash between England and Scotland?

207. Which Scottish defender did Paul Gascoigne beat for the second goal of their 2-0 victory in 1996?

208. Which player came on at half-time as a substitute for Stuart Pearce against Scotland in 1996 but was later replaced by Sol Campbell when he picked up an injury?

209. Who came on to score the only Dutch goal against England in 1996, sealing their move through to the quarter-finals and knocking out Scotland?

210. Alan Shearer scored two goals against Holland in Euro 96. Who scored the other two in their 4-1 victory?

196. Dean Saunders 197. **John Collins and Scott Booth** 198. Alan Shearer 199. **Kubilay Turkyilmaz** 200. Paul Ince 201. **Tony Adams** 202. Brian Laudrup, Ally McCoist and Paul Gascoigne 203. **Villa Park** 204. John Collins 205. **Tony Adams** 206. Gary McAllister 207. **Colin Hendry** 208. Jamie Redknapp 209. **Patrick Kluivert** 210. Teddy Sheringham

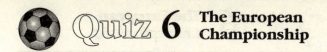

211. Who scored Scotland's only goal of the 1996 championships?

212. Which two players were sent off in the 1996 game between Spain and Bulgaria?

213. At which ground did France beat Romania 1-0 in Euro 96?

214. Who was the only man to score for Bulgaria in the 1996 championships?

215. What was the final score between France and Spain when they met in Euro 96?

216. Who scored Spain's winner against Romania to take them through to the 1996 quarter-finals?

217. Who was Germany's impressive full-back who scored against the Czech Republic in the group stages of Euro 96?

218. Who netted a brace for Italy against Russia in Euro 96, but was dropped from the starting line-up for the next game?

219. Who was the Italian manager whose tactical mistakes saw his team fail to qualify for the 1996 quarter-finals?

220. Which two teams did not win a single point in the 1996 championships?

221. What was the score in the 1996 tie between Croatia and Portugal?

222. Which England player was booked in their quarter-final clash with Spain in 1996, ruling him out of the semi-finals?

223. Which Spaniard's penalty hit the bar in their quarter-final clash with England in 1996?

224. Whose penalty did David Seaman save in England's quarter-final clash in 1996?

225. Who was the French goalkeeper who saved a penalty to take his team through to the 1996 semi-finals?

226. Which Croat player, who would later become familiar to Premiership spectators, was sent off in their quarter-final against Germany in 1996?

227. Which future Premiership player handled the ball to give Germany a penalty in their 1996 quarter-final against Croatia?

228. Who scored the Czech Republic's winner against Portugal in the 1996 quarter-finals?

229. Which English referee took part in Euro 96?

230. Who scored Germany's equaliser in their Euro 96 semi-final with England?

231. Which English player hit the post in their 1996 semi-final defeat at the hands of Germany?

232. Who was the German keeper who saved Gareth Southgate's penalty in the 1996 semi-final penalty shoot-out?

233. Who converted Germany's final penalty to take them through to the 1996 final?

234. Which French player's penalty was saved in the 1996 shoot-out against the Czech Republic?

235. Who scored the deciding penalty in the semi-final tie between the Czech Republic and France in 1996?

236. What was the attendance for the Euro 96 final at Wembley?

237. Who brought down Patrick Berger in the 1996 final for the Czech penalty?

238. Which German striker scored twice in the Euro 96 final?

239. Which team finished the 1996 tournament top of the Fair Play charts?

240. Which two countries have been chosen as hosts for the 2000 European Championships?

Quiz 7

F. A. Cup

1. **Who won the first FA Cup in 1871-72?**

2. Where was that game played?

3. **Who beat Derby County 6-0 to record the biggest FA Cup Final win?**

4. Which player has scored the most FA Cup goals this century?

5. **Who has made the most FA Cup appearances?**

6. Who is the youngest player to play in an FA Cup Final at Wembley?

7. **Name the youngest scorer in an FA Cup Final.**

8. Who is the oldest scorer in an FA Cup Final?

9. **Who is the youngest FA Cup Final captain?**

10. Who became the oldest player in the FA Cup, almost 20 years after scoring the winning goal for Manchester City in the Final?

11. **Who is the oldest player to play in an FA Cup Final?**

12. Who holds the record for most FA Cup wins?

13. **Who were the last team outside the top division to play in the FA Cup Final?**

14. Which was the only club to be relegated from the top flight after appearing in an FA Cup Final during the 1980's?

15. **Which team appeared in three successive finals in the 1990's?**

1. **The Wanderers** 2. The Kennington Oval 3. **Bury** 4. Ian Rush (Chester, Liverpool) 5. **Ian Callaghan (Liverpool, Swansea, Crewe)** 6. Paul Allen (West Ham United, 1980) 7. **Norman Whiteside (Manchester United, 1983)** 8. Bert Turner (Charlton Athletic, 1946) 9. **David Nish (Leicester City, 1969)** 10. Billy Meredith 11. **Walter Hampson (Newcastle, 1924)** 12. Manchester United 13. **Sunderland (1992)** 14. Brighton and Hove Albion (1983) 15. **Manchester United (1994,1995,1996)**

16. Which club lost successive Finals in the 1980's?

17. Which two players have made the most Finals appearances at Wembley (including replays)?

18. Which Sunderland player tied the record for most loser's medals in 1992?

19. Who was a winner with different clubs in successive 1970's Finals?

20. Who played for QPR in the 1982 Final against Tottenham and then for Tottenham in the 1987 Final?

21. Who scored for different teams in two of the first three Finals of the 1990's?

22. Who became the only on-loan player to play in the Final, winning with Manchester United in 1990?

23. Which father and son have both appeared in Final's with Tottenham?

24. Which Chile international played for Newcastle in the 1951 Final and scored the winning goal for them in the 1952 Final?

25. Which Belgian-born player made four Final appearances in six years?

26. Who was the first American to play in a Final?

27. Name the last three managers to have won the Cup as player and manager of the same club?

28. Who is the youngest manager of a Cup Final winning team?

29. Who is the only foreigner to captain his club to a Final win?

30. Who has scored the most goals in FA Cup Finals?

16. Everton (1985,19860) **17. Ray Clemence and Frank Stapleton** 18. Paul Bracewell (Everton 1985,1986,1989, Sunderland 1992) **19. Brian Talbot (Ipswich Town 1978, Arsenal 1979)** 20. Clive Allen **21. Ian Wright (Crystal Palace 1990, Arsenal 1993)** 22. Les Sealey **23. Les and Clive Allen** 24. George Robledo **25. Pat Van den Hauwe (Everton 1985,1986,1989, Tottenham 1991)** 26. John Harkes **27. Kenny Dalglish (Liverpool), Terry Venables (Tottenham), George Graham (Arsenal)** 28. Stan Cullis (Wolves, 1949) **29. Eric Cantona (Manchester United 1996) 30. Ian Rush (5)**

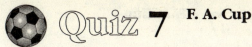
31. **Who scored the second fastest FA Cup Final goal at Wembley in 1955?**

32. Which Manchester United player made two substitute appearances in Finals while still a teenager?

33. **Who is the youngest goalkeeper to play in an FA Cup Final?**

34. Who are the only non-English club to win the FA Cup?

35. **Who was the last player to score in every round of the FA Cup in the same season?**

36. Since the Football League was formed, only one non-league club have won the Cup. Who are they?

37. **Who were the last non-league team to beat a side from the top flight?**

38. Which six teams have won the FA Cup and League Championship double?

39. **Who was the last team to be runners-up in the FA Cup and League Championship in the same year?**

40. Which Scottish club reached two FA Cup Finals?

41. **Which club entered the 1992-93 FA Cup but went into liquidation before playing a match?**

42. When was the last all-London FA Cup Final?

43. **When was the first all-Merseyside FA Cup Final?**

44. Which two teams played in the first semi-final to be staged at Wembley?

45. **Who became the first player to miss a penalty in the Final?**

31. Jackie Milburn (Newcastle United, 45 seconds) 32. David McCreery (Manchester United, 1976,1977) **33.** Peter Shilton (Leicester City, 1969) **34.** Cardiff City (1927) **35.** Peter Osgood (Chelsea, 1970) **36.** Tottenham Hotspur of the Southern League (1901) **37. Sutton United (v Coventry, 1989) 38.** Preston North End (1889), Aston Villa (1897), Tottenham (1961), Arsenal (1971), Liverpool (1986), **Manchester United (1994,1996) 39. Everton (1986) 40.** Queen's Park (1884,1885) **41. Maidstone United 42.** 1982 (Tottenham v QPR) **43.** 1986 **(Liverpool v Everton) 44.** Arsenal v Tottenham, 1991 **45. Charlie Wallace (Aston Villa, 1913)**

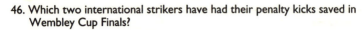

46. Which two international strikers have had their penalty kicks saved in Wembley Cup Finals?

47. And which two goalkeepers saved the kicks?

48. Which goalkeeper broke his neck in the 1956 Cup Final, but carried on playing to get a winners medal?

49. Which club has made the most semi-final appearances?

50. Who was the first player to be sent-off in the Final?

51. Who was the referee?

52. Who was the last man to be sent-off in an FA Cup semi-final?

53. Which four Nationwide League sides have reached three FA Cup semi-finals, and lost all of them?

54. Which two teams contested the lowest-attended semi-final in 1988?

55. Which ground has staged the most FA Cup semi-finals?

56. Which Chelsea player was refused a winners medal in 1970 because he was wearing a Leeds shirt he had exchanged after the whistle and an official believed he played for Leeds?

57. Which striker scored a hat-trick against West Bromwich for non-league Woking in 1991?

58. Which Cup winners are the only club to have beaten top-flight teams in every round?

59. Which Cup Final song reached number three in the charts in 1988?

60. Who were Hereford's scorers when the Southern League side beat Newcastle United 2-1 in a third round replay in 1972?

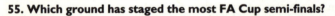

46. Liverpool's John Aldridge (1988), Tottenham's Gary Lineker (1991) 47. **Dave Beasant (Wimbledon, 1988), Mark Crossley (Nott'm. Forest, 1991)** 48. Bert Trautmann (Manchester City) 49. **Everton** 50. Kevin Moran (Manchester United, 1985) 51. **Peter Willis** 52. Lee Dixon (Arsenal, 1993) 53. **Millwall, Norwich City, Stoke City, Oldham Athletic** 54. Luton v Wimbledon 55. **Villa Park (45)** 56. David Webb 57. **Tim Buzaglo** 58. Manchester United (1948) 59. **Liverpool's "Anfield Rap"** 60. Ronnie Radford, Ricky George

61. Who was the scorer when Sunderland beat Leeds in the 1973 Cup Final?

62. Which Wimbledon goalkeeper saved Peter Lorimer's penalty in the fourth round draw with Leeds in 1975?

63. Who played for Manchester United in the Cup Final of 1979 against Arsenal, and then scored against the Londoners for Wrexham in 1992?

64. Which was the first club to win the Cup on three occasions?

65. Who was the first player to score a hat-trick in a Wembley FA Cup Final in 1953?

66. Who became the first player to score in successive FA Cup Finals at Wembley?

67. Who was the first substitute to appear in a Cup Final?

68. Who was the first substitute to score in the Final?

69. Which two substitutes scored twice when they came on in the 1989 Final?

70. Who were the last team to win the Cup with eleven English players?

71. When was the first FA Cup Final played at Wembley?

72. Who was the first person to win the Cup as player and manager of the same club?

73. Which two teams played in the first Wembley FA Cup Final that went to a replay?

74. What was the first Cup Final replay to be played at Wembley?

75. Which was the first Cup Final to produce gate receipts of £1 million?

61. Ian Porterfield 62. Dickie Guy **63. Mickey Thomas** 64. The Wanderers (1872,1873,1876) **65. Stan Mortensen (Blackpool)** 66. Bobby Johnstone (Manchester City, 1955,1956) **67. Derek Clarke (West Bromwich Albion, 1968)** 68. Eddie Kelly (Arsenal, 1971) **69. Stuart McCall (Everton), Ian Rush (Liverpool)** 70. West Ham (1975) **71. 1923** 72. Stan Seymour (Newcastle, 1924 (player), 1961,1952 (manager) **73. Chelsea and Leeds, 1970** 74. 1981, Tottenham v Manchester City **75. 1985, Manchester United v Everton**

76. Which two teams contested the first FA Cup tie to be decided on penalties in 1991?

77. **Which two teams became the first Cup Final sides to have the players' names on the back of their shirts?**

78. Who was the first black player to captain a Cup Final side?

79. **And which other black player captained the same side in the replay?**

80. Who was the first Premiership side to win the Cup?

81. **Who scored in Liverpool's 1992 FA Cup Final success and came on as a substitute in the 1996 Final?**

82. Who scored in the Manchester United v Brighton Final in 1983 and then played in the 1987 Final for Tottenham?

83. **Which Wigan player was carried off on a stretcher after 20 minutes of a 1965 first round replay against Doncaster Rovers but returned to the field to score a hat-trick?**

84. Who are the last non-league team to reach the Final?

85. **How many Final appearances have Bristol City made?**

86. Which team won the FA Cup in 1911, only eight years after forming?

87. **When was the last FA Cup Final played outside London?**

88. When was the last time both semi-finals were played at Wembley?

89. **Who were the first winners of the Littlewoods-sponsored FA Cup?**

90. What was the name of the white horse that pushed the crowds back in Wembley's first Cup Final?

76. Birmingham City v Stoke City, third place play-off, 1972. **77. Arsenal, Sheffield Wednesday, 1993 78.** Viv Anderson, Sheffield Wednesday, 1993 **79. Carlton Palmer 80.** Arsenal **81. Michael Thomas 82.** Gary Stevens **83. H.Lyons, 1965 84.** Southampton **85. One (1909) 86.** Bradford City **87. 1915 88.** 1994 **89. Everton, 1995 90.** Billy

91. **Which Nationwide League club are the only founder member of the Football League not to have won the FA Cup?**

92. Who were the first Football League club to win the FA Cup in 1889?

93. **William Townley was the first player to score a hat-trick in the Cup Final in 1890. But who did he play for?**

94. Who became the first non-league team to reach the Final?

95. **Who scored the first FA Cup Final goal at Wembley?**

96. Which club had to apply for re-election to the Football League, just seven years after winning the Cup?

97. **When was the first all-Lancashire FA Cup Final?**

98. What year did the Cup Final teams first wear numbers on their shirts?

99. **Which two Manchester City players won FA Cup medals in 1934, but were later in the Munich air crash of 1958?**

100. Name the referee of the 1934 Final who later became president of FIFA?

101. **Which former Liverpool manager played in Preston's 1938 FA Cup winning team?**

102. Which team has reached four FA Cup Finals, and have lost all of them?

103. **Portsmouth kept the Cup for seven years, but only reached the Final once. How come?**

104. Which London club played in successive Finals in the 1940's?

105. **Which team came from 3-1 down to beat Bolton 4-3 in the 1953 Final?**

91. **Stoke City** 92. Preston North End 93. **Blackburn Rovers** 94. Southampton, 1900 95. **David Jack (Bolton, 1923)** 96. Cardiff City 97. **1926 (Bolton v Manchester City)** 98. 1933 99. **Frank Swift and Sir Matt Busby** 100. Sir Stanley Rous 101. **Bill Shankly** 102. Leicester City 103. **They won in 1939, but the competition was suspended beacues of the Second World War.** 104. Charlton Athletic 105. **Blackpool**

106. How many loser's medals did Sir Stanley Matthews collect?

107. Which team scored 37 goals on their way to winning the Cup?

108. Which team won the Cup in the 1940's without playing a home tie?

109. Which non-league side failed to get into the first round just once between 1949 and 1972?

110. Who won the Cup three times in five years in the 1950's?

111. How many FA Cup Final appearances did George Best make?

112. How long did West Ham have to wait to make their second appearance in the Cup Final?

113. Which teams contested a third round tie that went to four replays in 1955?

114. Which goalkeeper broke his jaw after only six minutes in the 1957 Cup Final, but returned later as an outfield player?

115. When was the last of Bolton's FA Cup wins?

116. Who played in goal for Leicester City in the 1961 Cup Final against Tottenham?

117. Who were the last team to win successive FA Cup Finals?

118. Who scored the 100th Cup Final goal at Wembley?

119. Which two sides faced each other in three successive FA Cup ties each year between 1961 and 1963?

120. How many days did it take to play all the third round matches in 1963?

WHEN WAS THAT?

BOLTON WIN F.A. CUP

Daily blurb

121. Wembley stadium was refurbished for the 1966 World Cup Finals. But which two teams played the first FA Cup Final in the re-built stadium?

122. Which FA Cup Final scorer's father played with Sir Matt Busby in the Finals of 1933 and 1934?

123. Which two Manchester United players won the FA Cup in 1963, having been in the losing United sides of 1957 and 1958?

124. How many Midlands teams won the Cup betwen 1961 and 1997?

125. Who were the last team to come back from two goals down to win a Cup Final?

126. Which player, who did not have his name in the official programme, scored twice in the 1966 Final?

127. Which two former England goalkeepers played in losing Cup Finals for the same club in the 1960's?

128. Which teams played in the Centenary Final?

129. Who scored a last-minute penalty to give Arsenal a draw in the 1971 semi-final against Stoke?

130. Who played in goal for Tottenham in the 1981 Cup Final?

131. Which player was on the losing side in successive Finals before winning with Leeds in 1972?

132. Who were the first holders of the Cup to lose a Final at Wembley?

133. Which Cup Final was played on April 11th to help the England players prepare for the World Cup Finals?

134. Who scored twice when Colchester United beat Leeds in the fifth round in 1971?

135. Which team had their names on the back of their tracksuits before the 1961 Cup Final?

136. Which two-time FA Cup loser with Leicester City won the Cup with Arsenal in 1971?

137. Who is the highest-capped England player never to have won an FA Cup Final winners medal?

138. Which team appeared in three Finals in four years during the 1970's?

139. How many internationals were in Sunderland's Cup-winning side of 1973?

140. Who were the last team outside the top flight to win the Cup?

141. How many FA Cup matches did Fulham play in the 1974-75 season?

142. Which two former FA Cup winners were in the Fulham side in the 1975 Final?

143. Which FA Cup Final manager scored the winning goal for non-league Yeovil when they beat Sunderland in 1948?

144. Who was the first player to captain English and Scottish FA Cup winning teams?

145. Who lost an FA Cup Final as player in 1954, and as manager in 1967 and 1976 before winning the trophy with Manchester United?

146. Which Final-winning manager was an unused sub for West Ham in the 1975 Final?

147. Who scored Arsenal's late winner in the 1979 Final against Manchester United?

148. Who captained his side to three FA Cup triumphs at Wembley?

149. Who had to taken off suffering with 'sunstroke and emotion' after scoring an FA Cup Final winner?

150. Who scored Southampton's winning goal in the 1976 Final?

136. Frank McLintock 137. **Peter Shilton** 138. Leeds (1970,1972,1973) 139. **None** 140. West Ham, 1980 141. 12 142. Bobby Moore and Alan Mullery 143. **Alec Stock** 144. Martin Buchan (Aberdeen 1970) Manchester United (1977) 145. **Tommy Docherty** 146. Bobby Gould 147. **Alan Sunderland** 148. Bryan Robson (1983,1985,1990) 149. **Roger Osborne (Ipswich, 1978)** 150. Bobby Stokes

151. How many games did it take Arsenal to beat Liverpool in the FA Cup semi-final of 1980?

152. Who is the only player to play in five post-war FA Cup Finals for the same team?

153. Who was the Manchester City captain in their 1969 Cup success who later went on to become their manager?

154. Who scored both goals in the 1981 FA Cup Final?

155. Which club played in five FA Cup Finals from 1971 to 1980?

156. When Brighton reached the Cup Final in 1983 they beat Liverpool in the fifth round with a goal from a former Liverpool Cup Final goalscorer. Who was it?

157. Roy Dwight played for Nottingham Forest in the 1959 Final. His nephew was at Wembley for the 1984 Final. Who is he?

158. Who scored two Cup Final goals in three years in the 1980's?

159. Because of the Hillsborough disaster in 1989 the semi-final between Liverpool and Nottingham Forest was replayed at another ground. Where?

160. Which teams contested the 100th Cup Final?

161. Who is the only goalkeeper to captain his team in the Cup Final?

162. What was wrong with Tottenham's shirts in the 1987 Final?

163. Who played in six Cup Finals in Scotland before playing, and scoring, in the 1983 FA Cup Final?

164. Who scored for Coventry in the 1987 Final against the same club he had faced in another Final?

165. Who played for only the first two minutes of the 1982 Final for QPR before limping off injured?

166. Who made his last appearance for Tottenham in the 1987 Final?

167. Who captained Brighton in the 1983 Cup Final instead of suspended Steve Foster?

168. Which former Cup winner managed Crystal Palace to the Final in 1990?

169. Who scored an own goal in the 1991 Final?

170. Who became the first side to win a semi-final on penalties?

171. Who beat Cup holders Liverpool in a third round replay at Anfield in 1993?

172. Who scored Arsenal's winner in the semi-final against Tottenham in 1993?

173. Who invented the FA Cup?

174. Who was the first man to captain a winning side in successive Finals?

175. Who is the last Scotsman to captain an FA Cup winning side?

176. Which Russian goalkeeper played in a Cup Final?

177. Which Danish international played in the 1986, 1988 and 1992 FA Cup Finals?

178. Which striker played in the 1983 Final and later went on to become a football commentator for Spanish television?

179. Which two brothers played in the 1977 Final?

180. Who scored with a 20-yard volley in the 1981 Final replay?

166. Glenn Hoddle **167. Tony Grealish** 168. Steve Coppell **169. Des Walker (Nottingham Forest)** 170. Liverpool (1992) **171. Bolton Wanderers** 172. Tony Adams **173. Charles Alcock** 174. Danny Blanchflower (Tottenham, 1961, 1962) **175. Alan Hansen (Liverpool, 1986)** 176. Dmitri Kharine (Chelsea, 1974) **177. Jan Molby** 178. Michael Robinson (Brighton) **179. Brian and Jimmy Greenhoff** 180. Steve Mackenzie

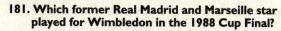

181. **Which former Real Madrid and Marseille star played for Wimbledon in the 1988 Cup Final?**

182. Who was the first Dutchman to play in an FA Cup Final?

183. **Who scored Manchester United's winner in the 1990 FA Cup Final replay?**

184. Who was the last club to lose in the Final, but succeed the following year?

185. **Who is the last player-manager to play in the Final?**

186. Who scored Arsenal's last minute winner in the 1993 Final replay?

187. **Apart from Ian Wright, who scored Crystal Palace's other goal in the 1990 Final?**

188. Who scored for both clubs in the 1987 Final?

189. **Who captained West Ham to FA Cup wins in 1975 and 1980?**

190. Which two players played in the 1968 Cup Final and then went on to win the FA Cup as managers of the same team?

191. **When did Luton Town last play in the FA Cup Final?**

192. Which two teams played out a 4-6 third round match in 1948?

193. **Who scored Crystal Palace's winning goal in their 4-3 semi-final win over Liverpool in 1990?**

194. Which two Everton strikers scored twice in a 4-4 fifth round replay against Liverpool in 1991?

195. **Which Cup Final featured two pairs of brothers on the field?**

181. **Laurie Cunningham** 182. Arnold Muhren (Manchester United,1983) 183. **Lee Martin** 184. Manchester United (1995,1996) 185. **Glenn Hoddle** (Chelsea,1994) 186. Andy Linighan 187. **Gary O'Reilly** 188. Gary Mabbutt 189. **Billy Bonds** 190. Howard Kendall and Joe Royle 191. 1959 192. Aston Villa and Manchester United 193. **Alan Pardew** 194. Graeme Sharp, Tony Cottee 195.

196. Has there ever been an FA Cup semi-final played outside England?

197. Which club's 4-0 victory at Brighton in 1973 was the biggest away win for a non-league side?

198. Who scored after just 45 seconds on his senior debut in an FA Cup tie in January 1953?

199. Which club played successive away ties in different rounds in the same season but on the same ground?

200. Which club reached a Cup Final after losing a game in the competition in the same season?

201. Who became the first player to play in the FA Cup for two different clubs in the same season?

202. Which Premiership team reached their first FA Cup semi-final in 1997?

203. Who were the last third division team, before Chesterfield in 1997, to reach the semi-finals?

204. Which team beat six Division One sides to FA Cup victory?

205. Who was refused a Cup winners medal from the royal box, and had it presented on the pitch after the official ceremony?

206. Which team collected a £30 clothing voucher as a bonus for winning the Cup?

207. Which Cup Final was dubbed "the Friendly Final"?

208. What was significant about J.F. Mitchell, who played in the 1922 Final for Preston?

209. When was the first FA Cup Final televised?

210. Which famous cricketer has a brother who played in the 1983 Final?

196. Yes. In Edinburgh in 1885 197. **Walton and Hersham** 198. Albert Taylor (Luton Town) 199. **Preston North End. They played Manchester City and Manchester United at Maine Road** 200. Charlton Athletic. They lost to Fulham in 1946 but the ties that season was played over two legs 201. **Jimmy Scoular in 1946 (Gosport and Portsmouth)** 202. Middlesbrough 203. **Plymouth Argyle** 204. Manchester United (1948) 205. **Kevin Moran (Manchester United, 1985)** 206. Everton (1933) 207. **Liverpool v Everton (1986)** 208. He wore glasses on the pitch 209. **1938** 210. Mike Gatting. His brother, Steve, played for Brighton and Hove Albion

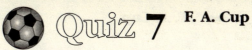

211. Which team took the FA Cup on their tour of South Africa in 1952?

212. Who asked for a transfer just an hour before the 1960 Final?

213. Which wine-bar waiter played in the 1987 semi-final?

214. Who scored for Oldham in the 1994 semi-final against Manchester United?

215. How many players did Mansfield Town have booked in their third round tie against Crystal Palace in 1963?

216. Which English club have played FA Cup ties in all three other home countries, against Linfield, Queen's Park and Cardiff City?

217. Who went 16 matches without a win in the competition, from February 1952 to March 1963?

218. The official record attendance for an FA Cup tie is 126,047. What year?

219. Which team reached two successive Finals without being drawn at home?

220. Which three England World Cup winners have never played in an FA Cup Final?

221. Which England player played his last game for his club in an FA Cup Final, and was stretchered off after only 16 minutes?

222. Who scored for Sutton United in their 2-1 third round victory over Coventry in 1989?

223. Who beat Sutton 8-0 in the following round?

224. Who was sent-off in Manchester United's semi-final replay against Crystal Palace in 1995?

225. Who was sent-off for West Ham in the 1991 semi-final against Nottingham Forest?

226. Who scored Arsenal's consolation goal in their 3-1 semi-final defeat against Tottenham in 1991?

227. Which Footballer of the Year captained his side to victory in the 1964 Final?

228. Which goalkeeper replaced Gary Sprake for Leeds' 1970 Final replay?

229. Who scored both of West Ham's goals in the 1975 Final?

230. Who scored the winning goal for York City against Arsenal in 1985, and scored in the Cup Final two years later?

231. Which non-league team celebrated scoring goals by waddling along the ground like ducks?

232. Who did Arsenal beat 3-0 in the semi-final of 1978?

233. Which London club won in their first FA Cup Final in the 1980's?

234. Who became the first player this century to play in three FA Cup Finals against the same club?

235. How many goal-less FA Cup Finals have there been at Wembley?

236. Name the last two players to be voted Footballer of the Year and captain an FA Cup winning side?

237. What have Sir Stanley Matthews, Harry Johnston, Nat Lofthouse, Tom Finney, Don Revie, Syd Owen, Jimmy Adamson, Bobby Collins, Billy Bremner, Alan Mullery, Emlyn Hughes, Neville Southall, Gary Lineker, Clive Allen, John Barnes and Chris Waddle all got in common?

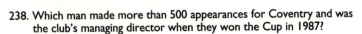

238. Which man made more than 500 appearances for Coventry and was the club's managing director when they won the Cup in 1987?

239. Which player lost two front teeth after colliding with a team-mate in the 1981 Final?

240. Who beat Hyde FC 26-0 in 1887 for the biggest win in FA Cup history?

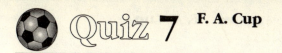

241. Who scored Chelsea's goal in the 1996 semi-final at Villa Park?

242. Which of the Neville brothers came on as a sub in the 1996 FA Cup Final?

243. Who scored Everton's winner in the 1995 Final?

244. Which two England goalkeepers played in the 1993 Final?

245. Who finished a 20-year association with Arsenal by winning his second FA Cup winners medal?

246. Who scored Manchester United's second goal in a 3-0 fourth round win at Reading in 1996?

247. Liverpool conceded only one goal on their way to the 1996 Final. Who scored against them?

248. Up to the 1997 Final, which Premiership club hasn't beaten Manchester United in the FA Cup for 76 years?

249. Who scored Wimbledon's winner in their 1988 semi-final against Luton?

250. Which two teams met twice in four years in FA Cup semi-finals in the 1990's?

251. Who held Brighton to a 2-2 draw in the first round in 1995?

252. Who did Fulham beat 7-0 in the first round in 1995?

253. By what scoreline did Oxford United beat Dorchester in the first round of 1995?

254. How many goals were scored in the 1995-96 first round tie between Shrewsbury and Marine?

255. Name the last Fourth Division club to reach the quarter-finals.

256. What year was it?

257. Who has made three appearances in the Final for Tottenham and one for Chelsea in the space of 13 years?

258. Tony Philliskirk scored five goals in a first round tie against Kingstonian in 1992, but does not have it officially recognised because the game was abandoned. Who was he playing for?

259. Which former president of the FA appeared in nine of the first 12 FA Cup Finals?

260. Which three former Liverpool players have all won three Cup winners' medals with the club?

261. What was the amazing feat of all 12 Manchester United players who played in the 1985 Final?

262. Only once in the competition's history have all the quarter-finals been won by the away teams. In which season?

263. Has there ever been an FA Cup Final where the top division was not represented?

264. Which club, in 1994-95, was originally banned from the competition but re-admitted on appeal?

265. Who scored Chesterfield's only goal in their 1996-97 quarter-final win over Wrexham?

266. Which Premiership club beat Blackburn in the fourth round of the 1996-97 season?

267. Who scored a last-minute own goal to send the fifth round tie between Leicester and Chelsea to a replay in 1996-97?

268. Who defeated Leeds at Elland Road to win a place in the 1996-97 quarter-finals?

269. Chelsea came back from 2-0 down at half-time to beat Liverpool in the 1996-97 fourth round. Who scored twice for the Londoners?

270. Which Hull City striker scored six goals in a first round replay against Whitby Town in the 1996-97 season?

270. Duane Darby

267. **Chelsea's Eddie Newton** 268. Portsmouth 269. **Gianluca Vialli**
266. **Chris Beaumont** 265. Tottenham 264. **No** 263. Coventry
als 262. 1986-87 261. **They were all internation-**
260. Ian Rush, Bruce Grobbelaar and Steve Nicol
256. 1990 257. **Glenn Hoddle** 258. Peterborough United 259. **James Forrest**

1. **Who was the first 'Footballer of the Year'?**

2. Who was the first 'Manager of the Year' in 1966?

3. **Which was the first game to be broadcast on 'Match of the Day'?**

4. Who were the first team to achieve the 'double'?

5. **Who was the first man to hit 60 League goals in a season?**

6. Who was the first player in British football to score a 'golden goal'?

7. **Which club were the first to concede and score 100 League goals in one season?**

8. Who was the first player to notch up a century of England appearances?

9. **Who was the first player to notch up a century of Scotland appearances?**

10. Who was the first player to notch up a century of Northern Ireland appearances?

11. **Where was the first indoor World Cup game?**

12. Who were England's opponents for the first all-seated football international at Wembley?

13. **Who was the first black player to win a full England cap?**

14. Who was the first black player to captain England at full international level?

15. **Who was the first man to play in and then manage League Championship-winning teams?**

16. Which club was first to be relegated from the Football League in 1923?

17. **In what year were the Division Three North and South replaced by Divisions Three and Four?**

18. In which year was the Premier League created?

19. **Who was the first player to reach 1000 League appearances when he played for Leyton Orient in 1996?**

20. Which Manchester City keeper became the first to play in all four divisions in one season in 1986/87?

21. **Who were the first club to take the FA Cup out of England?**

22. Who is the only man to score a hat-trick in a post-war FA Cup final?

23. **In what year was the hymn 'Abide With Me' introduced as part of the FA Cup Final build-up?**

24. Who was the first guest of honour at the FA Cup final of 1923?

25. **Who was the first player sent off playing for England?**

26. In what year did Walter Winterbottom become the first official manager of England?

27. **Who was the first manager to win the League Championship with two different clubs when he led both Huddersfield and Arsenal to the title?**

28. Who was the first man to become a player-manager in the top flight when he took over QPR in 1968?

29. **In which year was the first FA Cup final at Wembley Stadium?**

30. In which year was the first Wembley game played under floodlights?

31. Who scored the first 'golden goal' which decided a major international tournament?

32. In which year was the first penalty scored in a first-class match?

33. Which club was the first in competitive British football to win a game through a penalty shoot-out?

34. Who became the first player to miss an FA Cup final penalty at Wembley when he failed to convert in 1988?

35. Who was the first player to score 200 goals in the Scottish Premier League?

36. Who were the first British club to play in Europe?

37. When did the Scottish First Division become the Premier League?

38. In which year were the first shinguards used?

39. In which year was professionalism in the game legalised?

40. In which year did the white ball come into official use?

41. In which year were substitutes introduced into Football League matches?

THE LATEST THING

42. The 'three points for a win' system was introduced by the Football League in which year?

43. When was the 'professional foul' made a sending-off offence?

44. When was the 'backpass' rule put into operation?

45. In which year was the numbering of Football League shirts made compulsory?

31. Oliver Bierhoff (Euro 96 final) 32. 1891 33. Manchester United (Watney Cup semi-final v Hull in 1970) 34. John Aldridge 35. Ally McCoist 36. Hibernian in 1955/56 37. 1975 38. 1874 39. 1885 40. 1951 41. 1965 42. 1981 43. 1990 44. 1992 45. 1939

46. Two substitutes were permitted in League games from which year?

47. **Who was the first substitute to score in an FA Cup final?**

48. In which year was the ceiling for footballers' earnings abolished?

49. **Who was the first British footballer to earn £100 a week?**

50. Who became the first sponsors of the Football League in 1983?

51. **Which club was the first to install an artificial pitch, in 1981?**

52. Which year saw the end of artificial turf pitches in the First Division?

53. **According to the original Taylor Report, when were all Premier League and First Division stadia required to become all-seater?**

54. When was the FA's School of Excellence at Lilleshall opened?

55. **Leyton Orient player Terry Howard hit the headlines when he lost his job in Feb 1995. Why?**

56. Which was the first football match to be televised in its entirety?

57. **What was introduced in Jan 1963 after a spell of particularly bad weather?**

58. Who were the first Olympic Games football champions in 1908?

59. **In which year was the first football code of laws compiled?**

60. The foundation of the Football Association occurred in which year?

46. 1987 47. **Eddie Kelly (Arsenal v Liverpool, 1971)** 48. 1961 49. **Johnny Haynes** 50. Canon 51. **QPR** 52. 1991 53. **August 1994** 54. 1984 55. **First recorded instance of a player being sacked at half-time.** 56. Arsenal 3 Everton 2 (August 1936) 57. **Pools Panel** 58. Great Britain 59. **1848** 60. 1863

61. Who did England play in the first official international in 1872?

62. The referee's job was made a little easier with what 1878 introduction?

63. In which year were goal nets introduced?

64. Which country did England play in the first Wembley international?

65. In 1935 trials were held for which innovation in football discipline?

66. Which was the first club to complete a hat-trick of consecutive League titles?

67. In which year was the first live television transmission of an FA Cup Final?

68. Who were the first foreign team to beat England in a full international at Wembley?

69. The last Football League Christmas Day programme was completed in which year?

70. The system of loan transfers was introduced in which year?

71. A decision by the PFA in 1978 precipitated which introduction into English football?

72. A European ban on all English clubs was introduced in which year?

73. Who, in 1986, became the first club to ban visiting supporters?

74. The system of play-off matches for promotion and relegation was introduced in which year?

75. Which English club was the last to revert to grass from artificial pitches?

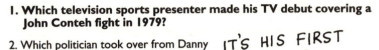

Quiz 9   The Commentators

1. **Which television sports presenter made his TV debut covering a John Conteh fight in 1979?**

2. Which politician took over from Danny Baker as the presenter of Radio Five Live's Six-O-Six programme?

3. **Which television sports presenter hosted a holiday programme?**

4. Which former Tottenham and Manchester United player now works for the BBC?

5. **Which former England international is the main summariser for the BBC?**

6. Who hosts ITV's sports programme 'Do I Not Like That'?

7. **Which two Premiership managers worked for the BBC during Euro '96?**

8. Which former England international now has his own show on BBC Radio Five Live?

9. **Whose has commentated on football for the BBC since 1971?**

10. Who commentated on his first World Cup Final in 1994?

11. **Which former Liverpool and Scotland striker works for ITV Sport?**

12. Which former Newcastle manager is a regular summariser on ITV?

13. **Who is the former Luton and Leicester manager who works for BBC?**

14. Which former England international worked on the BBC's coverage of Newcastle's 1996-97 Uefa Cup campaign?

15. **Which two former internationals had a long-running Saturday luchtime show on ITV?**

1. **Desmond Lynam** 2. David Mellor 3. **Desmond Lynam** 4. Garth Crooks 5. **Trevor Brooking** 6. Richard Littlejohn 7. **Ruud Gullit and David Pleat** 8. Gary Lineker 9. **John Motson** 10. Barry Davies 11. **Ian St John** 12. Kevin Keegan 13. **David Pleat** 14. Chris Waddle 15. **Ian St John and Jimmy Greaves**

16. What was the show called?

17. Who hosts Channel Four's Football Italia?

18. Which former commentator also works on Football Italia?

19. Which former BBC commentator now works for satellite channel Eurosport?

20. Which former England international works for ITV, Channel Four and Sky Sports?

21. Who is Sky Sports' main football commentator?

22. Who took over from Desmond Lynam as the presenter of BBC's Grandstand?

23. Who is the host of Grandstand's Football Focus?

24. Who is Channel Four's main commentator for Football Italia?

25. Which former Scotland striker appears on Channel Four's Football Italia?

26. Who was the original host of Radio Five Live's 'Six-O-Six' programme?

27. Who is Sky Sports' top football presenter?

28. Who is Sky Sports' main summariser, and also has a column in The Express newspaper?

29. Which sports presenter turned down the chance to stand-in for Terry Wogan on his chat-show?

30. Name the former Watford striker who appears on Channel Four's Football Italia?

16. Saint and Greavsie' 17. **Gary Richardson** 18. Kenneth Wolstenholme 19. **Archie McPherson** 20. Ray Wilkins 21. **Martin Tyler** 22. Steve Rider 23. **Gary Lineker** 24. Peter Brackley 25. **Joe Jordan** 26. Danny Baker 27. **Richard Keys** 28. Andy Gray 29. **Desmond Lynam** 30. Luther Blissett

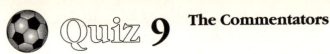
31. **Which international manager worked for ITV during Euro '96?**

32. Who presents BBC's Sport on Friday programme?

33. **Which woman personality presents Sky's Goals on Sunday programme?**

34. Which former Page Three model hosts a sports programme on Channel Five?

35. **Which former Pisa defender works on Channel Four's Football Italia?**

36. Which former footballer is a team captain in BBC's television quiz 'They Think It's All Over'?

37. **Which television commentator's middle name is Baden?**

38. Which television commentator was a director at Gillingham from 1977 to 1985?

39. **Which comedian presented the nostalgia football show 'There's Only One Brian Moore'?**

40. Which football pundit is a former head of sport at London Weekend Television?

41. **Which international manager worked for the BBC in the 1994 World Cup?**

42. Which former Brighton and Liverpool striker moved to Spain and became a commentator after his playing days?

43. **Which former England captain works for BBC Radio Five Live?**

44. Fantasy Football League's 'Statto' also commentates for Eurosport. What is his real name?

45. **In which year did Bob Wilson defect from BBC to ITV?**

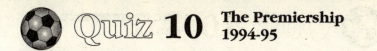

1. **The first goal of the season comes at Highbury, where Arsenal are playing Manchester City. Who is the scorer?**

2. Which German scores his first Premiership goal at Sheffield Wednesday on the first day of the season?

3. **Which team do Liverpool beat 6-1 on the opening day of the season?**

4. In the draw between Newcastle and Leicester City in August which player suffers a cheek-bone fracture?

5. **Which £5m player scores his first for Blackburn in August against Leicester City?**

6. Which German scores a brace in Manchester City's 4-0 win over Everton in August?

7. **Which team went top after three games and three victories?**

8. Who scores a four-and-a-half minute hat-trick for Liverpool when they beat Arsenal 3-0 in August?

9. **Which club went top of the Premiership for a day in August?**

10. Which team begins the season with the prospect of having six points deducted?

11. **Which captain is sent off in Wimbledon's 2-1 win over Leicester in September?**

12. Which player scores seven goals in his first six games in the Premiership?

13. **Who scores Arsenal's own goal in Newcastle's 3-2 win in September?**

14. **Which ex-Tottenham player scores the winner as Ipswich pull off a shock victory over Manchester United in September?**

15. **Who hit a hat-trick for Liverpool as they trounce Sheffield Wednesday in September?**

1. **Kevin Campbell** 2. Jurgen Klinsmann 3. **Crystal Palace** 4. Peter Beardsley 5. **Chris Sutton** 6. Uwe Rosler 7. **Newcastle United** 8. Robbie Fowler 9. **Nottingham Forest** 10. Tottenham Hotspur 11. **Vinnie Jones** 12. Jurgen Klinsmann 13. **Martin Keown** 14. Steve Sedgeley 15. **Steve McManaman**

16. Which player scores his 100th goal for Arsenal in October?

17. Who is sent off when Blackburn meet Manchester United in October?

18. Who are the only club in Britain without a win after 12 games?

19. Which club ends Newcastle's unbeaten run at the end of October?

20. Which club ends Nottingham Forest's unbeaten run on the same day?

21. Which foreigner's goal at Villa Park in November lifts Manchester United to third in the table?

22. Which three managers get the sack at the beginning of November?

23. Which player scores a hat-trick in November as Manchester United's set their biggest derby win in history?

24. At White Hart Lane in November Tottenham fight back against Aston Villa from 3-0 down only to lose to a last-minute winner. Who scored that goal?

25. Which on-loan striker scores for Everton in their first win of the season in the Liverpool derby?

26. Who scores a hat-trick as Blackburn go top in November after a 4-0 win over QPR?

27. Who scores a hat-trick for Tottenham as they produce a 4-2 win at home to Newcastle in December?

28. Which two strikers net a brace in Manchester United's 3-2 win over QPR in December?

29. Which team are the first of the season to beat Manchester United at Old Trafford when they win 2-1 in December?

30. Which team set a club record seven games without a goal in a goalless draw at home to Tottenham in December?

16. Ian Wright **17. Henning Berg** 18. Everton **19. Manchester United** 20. **Blackburn 21. Andrei Kanchelskis** 22. Ossie Ardiles, Mike Walker and Ron Atkinson **23. Andrei Kanchelskis** 24. Dean Saunders **25. Duncan Ferguson** 26. Alan Shearer **27. Teddy Sheringham** 28. Les Ferdinand and Paul Scholes **29. Nottingham Forest** 30. Everton

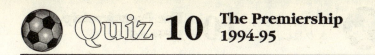

31. **Which Sheffield Wednesday new boy scores twice on his debut at Everton on Boxing Day?**

32. In Manchester United's Boxing Day clash with Chelsea, who scores the winner in their 3-2 victory?

33. **Who scores his first goal in his 98th match for Arsenal in December?**

34. Blackburn achieve a six-point lead in the Premiership at the start of January with a hat-trick from which player against West Ham?

35. **The North London derby at White Hart Lane ends 1-0. Who is sent off for Arsenal?**

36. Ipswich record their first-ever win at Anfield thanks to a goal from which player?

37. **Which Manchester United player scores but is then stretchered off when they play Newcastle in January?**

38. The battle of the top two clubs, Manchester United and Blackburn, is resolved with a goal from which player in January?

39. **Which two Hammers are dismissed when they meet Sheffield Wednesday in January?**

40. Which South African international scores two goals as Leeds beat QPR 4-0 in January?

41. **Which goalkeeper is sent off after only two minutes in a game against Leeds in February?**

42. In February, which Everton player is sent off on his debut?

43. **Which Manchester United player scores his first goal for the club in a 1-0 victory over Aston Villa in February?**

44. What was the scoreline when Blackburn are beaten by Tottenham in February, losing the chance of stretching their lead to five points?

45. **Who hits a hat-trick as Aston Villa put seven past Wimbledon in February?**

31. **Guy Whittingham** 32. Brian McClair 33. **John Jensen** 34. Alan Shearer 35. **Stefan Schwarz** 36. Adam Tanner 37. **Mark Hughes** 38. Eric Cantona 39. **Alvin Martin and Tim Breacker** 40. Phil Masinga 41. **Tim Flowers** 42. Earl Barrett 43. **Andy Cole** 44. 3-1 45. **Tommy Johnson**

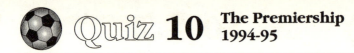
46. Which Arsenal player breaks a leg in the 1-1 draw with Leicester in February?

47. **Which goalkeeper is sent off when Blackburn beat Sheffield Wednesday 3-1 in February to reclaim their place at the top of the league.**

48. Who scores his first goal for Arsenal when they beat Nottingham Forest in February?

49. **Which club scores three goals in the last 13 minutes at Villa Park in February to take themselves off the bottom of the table?**

50. Who scores his first goal for Leeds in February when they beat Everton 1-0 at home?

51. **A goal from which player gives Everton an unexpected win at home to Manchester United in February?**

52. How many goals do Manchester United put past Ipswich in March to establish a Premiership record?

53. **Which player scores five goals in that game?**

54. Which two Everton men are sent off when the Toffeemen squander a two-goal lead at Leicester in March?

55. **Joe Kinnear is ordered from the bench in a game against Manchester United in March when which player is sent off?**

56. Which Coventry player scores a hat-trick as they beat Liverpool 3-2 in March?

57. **Against which club does Alan Shearer score his 100th league goal in March?**

58. Which player scores an own goal as Liverpool beat Manchester United 2-0 in March?

59. **Which two Nottingham Forest players score six goals in two games to lift their club to fourth in March?**

60. Which team beat Sheffield Wednesday 7-1 to give the Owls their biggest-ever home defeat in April?

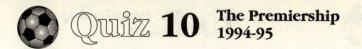
61. Who scores the winner for Southampton in their seven-goal thriller with Tottenham in April?

62. What is the biggest points lead which Blackburn attain over Manchester United?

63. Whose Leeds hat-trick condemns Ipswich to the bottom of the table in April and confimed relegation a week later?

64. Whose late Tottenham equaliser denies Crystal Palace three vital points in April?

65. Whose last-minute equaliser for Leeds against Blackburn helps Manchester United to cut the gap to six points with five games remaining?

66. Which team brings an end to Newcastle's 15-month unbeaten run at St James' Park?

67. Who scores the winner for Manchester City when they beat Blackburn in April?

68. Who beats Leicester 2-0 in April to condemn the Foxes to relegation?

69. Blackburn beat Palace 2-1 in April to restore their eight-point lead. Neither Shearer or Sutton scores, but who does?

70. Who scores his 28th goal of the season in the North London derby at Highbury in April?

71. After defeat against which club do angry Norwich fans protest, leading to 13 arrests, in April?

72. Which team beats Blackburn 2-0 at the end of April to keep the championship race alive?

73. Who scores a brace for Manchester United on May 1 in their win over Coventry to close the gap to five points?

74. Whose last-minute goal for Leeds gave them a win over Norwich which relegates the Canaries?

75. A goal from which player gives Manchester United a win over Sheffield Wednesday, closing the gap at the top?

Quiz 10

76. Who do Blackburn beat to restore their five-point lead at the top?

77. Who scores the penalty to give Manchester United a victory at home to Southampton and a gap of only two points with one game to play?

78. Who beats Blackburn on the last day of the season?

79. Who scores the West Ham goal which ultimately denies Manchester United the title?

80. Which team beats Crystal Palace on the last day of the season to condemn the Eagles to relegation?

81. Which team finishes one positition above the relegation places?

82. Which team finishes in third behind Blackburn and Manchester United?

83. What is the final points gap between the top two teams?

84. Which two players were sent off in the game between QPR and Manchester United in August, the first dismissals of the Premiership season?

85. How many managers lose their jobs throughout the season?

86. Which Crystal Palace player receives a ban after testing positive for cannabis?

87. Which referee revokes his decision to send off Alvin Martin in West Ham's game with Sheffield Wednesday?

88. Which club are hit by allegations of 'bungs' in their transfer dealings with Scandinavian clubs?

89. Which player retires but then returns at the age of 38 when his team face possible relegation?

90. At which unlikely venue did Jurgen Klinsmannn announce that he will play only one season in England?

76. Newcastle United 77. **Denis Irwin** 78. Liverpool 79. **Michael Hughes** 80. Newcastle United 81. **Aston Villa** 82. Nottingham Forest 83. **One point** 84. Clive Wilson and Paul Parker 85. **12** 86. Chris Armstrong 87. **Paul Danson** 88. Arsenal 89. **Gordon Strachan** 90. The Comedy Cafe

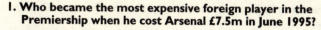

1. **Who became the most expensive foreign player in the Premiership when he cost Arsenal £7.5m in June 1995?**

2. Which Belgian international played a season with Sheffield Wednesday in 1995-96?

3. **At one time Middlesbrough had three Brazilians in their squad. Can you name them?**

4. Which midfielder was shortlighted as PFA Young Player of the Year in his first season in England?

5. **Which former Middlesbrough striker played in the 1994 World Cup Finals?**

6. Which foreign striker is nicknamed 'The White Feather'?

7. **For how much did Swedish midfielder Tomas Brolin join Leeds for?**

8. Which club did he sign from?

9. **Who were the two Argentinians that arrived at Tottenham after the 1978 World Cup Final?**

10. Which two Italian clubs did Chelsea's Ruud Gullit play for?

11. **Which two European strikers were part of Tottenham manager Ossie Ardiles' Fab Five?**

12. Who was the Romanian midfielder at Tottenham during 1994-95?

13. **How many of Norway's 1994 World Cup squad were playing their football in England at the time of the Finals?**

14. Patrick Vieira is just one one of three French players to play at Arsenal in 1996-97. Name the other two.

15. **Which foreign player broke Aston Villa's transfer record when he signed for £3.5m in June 1995?**

1. **Dennis Bergkamp** 2. Marc Degryse 3. **Juninho, Emerson, Branco** 4. Patrick Vieira 5. **Jan-Aage Fjortoft** 6. Fabrizio Ravanelli 7. **£4.5m** 8. Parma 9. **Ossie Ardiles and Ricky Villa** 10. AC Milan, Sampdoria 11. **Jurgen Klinsmann and Ilie Dumitrescu** 13. **10** 14. Remi Garde and Nicolas Anelka 12. Gica Popescu 15. Savo Milosevic

Quiz 11 — Foreign Players In England

16. Who moved to England just four days after lifting the European Cup for Juventus?

17. Australian Mark Bosnich was at another Premiership club before Aston Villa. What club was it?

18. Where did Blackburn buy Lars Bohinen from?

19. Which Zimbabwean played for Coventry in 1996-97?

20. How much did Gianfranco Zola cost Chelsea when he moved from Parma?

21. Which Blackburn player played in a 1996 European Cup semi-final?

22. What nationality is Chelsea goalkeeper Frode Grodas?

23. Name the former clubs of Chelsea's Dan Petrescu?

24. Where did Middlesbrough buy Mikkel Beck from?

25. What nationality is Sasa Curcic?

26. Name the Aston Villa defender from Portugal?

27. Dwight Yorke plays for which country?

28. Where did Blackburn buy Henning Berg from?

29. Who was Chelsea's Danish defender in the 1994 FA Cup Final?

30. Derby had a Danish defender in 1996-97. Who is he?

16. Gianluca Vialli 17. **Manchester United** 18. Nottingham Forest 19. **Peter Ndlovu** 20. £4.5m 21. **Georgios Donis** 22. Norwegian 23. **Steaua Bucharest, Foggia, Genoa and Sheffield Wednesday** 24. Fortuna Cologne 25. **Serbian** 26. Fernando Nelson 27. **Trinidad and Tobago** 28. Lillestrom 29. **Jakob Kjeldbjerg** 30. Jacob Laursen

31. **Which Chelsea player formerly played for Bayern Munich?**

32. Which Russian winger joined Everton for £5million in August 1995?

33. **Which USA '94 star joined Tottenham from Steaua Bucharest for £2.6million?**

34. Who cost Arsenal £1.75million when he joined them in 1994 from Benfica?

35. **Marc Hottiger played for Everton in 1996-97. Which other English club had he previously played for?**

36. Name the two players who joined Sheffield Wednesday from RS Belgrade in 1995.

37. **How much did Chelsea pay for Italian international Roberto Di Matteo?**

38. And from which club did they buy him from?

39. **Which Czech Republic star joined Manchester United from Slavia Prague in 1996?**

40. How much did he cost?

41. **Which two South Africans played for Leeds United in 1995-96?**

42. From which club did Leeds buy Tony Yeboah from?

43. **Which midfielder did Coventry buy from Benfica?**

44. Which Croation defender joined Derby in 1995?

45. **From which club did he come from?**

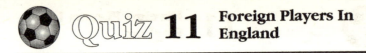

46. Another Croation international joined Derby in 1996. Name him.

47. From which club did Everton buy Daniel Amokachi in 1994?

48. What country does Amokachi represent?

49. Which Norwegian international defender did Liverpool buy from Rosenborg?

50. Name the Dutch goalkeeper who signed for Manchester United in 1996.

51. From which club did he come from?

52. Ronnie Johnsen joined Manchester United in 1996. Where from?

53. Phillipe Albert joined Newcastle in 1994. From which club?

54. And how much did he cost Newcastle?

55. Which foreigner won consecutive championships with different English clubs?

56. Who were Manchester United playing on the night of Eric Cantona's infamous "kung-fu kick"?

57. Jordi Cruyff joined Manchester United from which club?

58. Name the Manchester United star who joined them from Norwegian side Molde?

59. Which Swedish winger has played for two Premiership sides?

60. Which Italian side did he play for before joining Arsenal?

61. Where did Newcastle buy Colombian international Faustino Asprilla from?

62. And how much did he cost?

63. David Ginola came to Tyneside from which French side?

64. Name the Croatian player who joined Nottingham Forest from Spanish side Real Ovieda?

65. Who became the first Italian to play in the Premiership?

66. From which club did Nottingham Forest buy him from?

67. Another player joined Forest from Serie A in 1994. Who was he?

68. How much did he cost?

69. From which club did Aston Villa buy midfielder Sasa Curcic from?

70. How much did they pay for him?

71. Who was the first foreigner to captain a side in the FA Cup Final?

72. Which World Cup star did West Ham buy from Espanol for £2.4million?

73. Newcastle had a Czech Republic player in their 1996-97 squad. Who is he?

74. Which Frenchman joined Chelsea in 1996?

75. Which foreign player scored the Premiership's first hat-trick of the 96-97 season?

61. Parma 62. £6.7m 63. Paris St Germain 64. Nikola Jerkan 65. Andrea Silenzi 66. Torino 67. Brian Roy 68. £2.5m 69. Bolton 70. £4m 71. Eric Cantona 72. Florin Raducioiu 73. Pavel Srnicek 74. Franck Leboeuf 75. Fabrizio Ravanelli

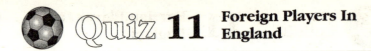
76. Against which team did Fabrizio Ravanelli score his first Premiership goal?

77. Which two English clubs has defender Ken Monkou played for?

78. Which country did he come from?

79. Name the Israeli international who plays for Totenham.

80. Name the Icelandic international who played for Bolton in 1996-97?

81. For which other English club has he played for?

82. Which Croatian defender joined West Ham from German club Karlsruhe in 1995?

83. Name the Danish defender who played in Euro '96 and played for West Ham in 1996-97?

84. Who joined West Ham from AC Milan in the summer of 1996?

85. Which Manchester United players former clubs are Hvidovre and Brondby?

86. Which Premiership player scored in the Euro 96 final?

87. Name the Australian who joined West Ham from West Adelaide.

88. Name the Norwegian who played for Wimbledon in 1996-97.

89. Which country does Liverpool goalkeeper Michael Stensgaard come from?

90. How much did Jurgen Klinsmann cost Tottenham?

91. Against which club did Klinsmann score his first Premiership goal?

92. Which Wimbledon midfielder was signed from Rosenberg?

93. Name the American goalkeeper who signed for Luton Town from West Ham in 1995.

94. Which Dutch defender moved to Sheffield United from Man.City in 1995?

95. Name the former Liverpool player who became player-manager of Swansea City in 1995-96.

96. Sheffield Wednesday paid £275,000 for a Dutch winger in 1996. Who was he?

97. From which club did he sign from?

98. Name the Dutch midfielder who has played for both Bolton and WBA?

99. From which country did Manchester City sign Mikhail Kavelashvili in March 1996?

100. How much did they pay for him?

101. Jorge Cadette joined Celtic in March '96. From which club?

102. What was the fee?

103. Name the two Swedish midfielders who joined Bolton in the summer of 1996.

104. Which Serie A player joined Glasgow Rangers in July 1996?

105. Name the only member of Portugals' Euro '96 squad to play in the 1996-97 Premiership.

106. Which Danish international joined Tottenham for a fee of £1.65million?

107. From which club did he sign?

108. Name the Bolivian international who left the Premiership to join Washington DC

109. Name the Zimbabwe international who joined Plymouth in August 1996.

110. Which Belgium player joined Coventry for a fee of £1million in August 1996?

111. From which club did Tottenham sign Norwegian goalkeeper Espen Baardsen?

112. Which Liverpool star helped the Czech Republic qualify for Euro '96 with four goals in qualifying?

113. Which Manchester United star is nicknamed "the express train"?

114. Which Danish defender returned home after two unsuccessful seasons at Liverpool under Graeme Souness?

115. Name the Everton star who was part of the Danish Euro '96 squad.

116. Which Russsian international played for Chelsea in 1996-97?

117. Name the Swiss International who cost Tottenham £3.75million.

118. From which club did he sign?

119. Which Manchester United player is known as "The Milkman"?

120. Name the former Torino player who joined Grimsby in August 1996.

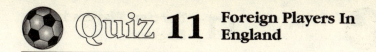

121. Which former Serie A star left Glasgow Rangers in the summer of 1996?

122. Name the French midfielder who joined Arsenal from AC Milan in August 1995?

123. Which American player has played for Milwall and Leicester?

124. Who did Egil Ostenstadt sign for in October '96?

125. Name the Israeli midfielder who also joined Southampton in the same month.

126. Name the Aston Villa player who scored a hat-trick in the World Cup Qualifying win against the Faroe Islands.

127. Which Blackburn player scored Greece's only goal in the 2-1 defeat by Demark in a World Cup Qualifying game in October '96?

128. Name the Croatian defender who helped Croatia to a 4-1 victory over Bosnia in the same month.

129. Which former West Ham player scored two goals in Ajax's 4-1 Champions League game against Rangers in 1996?

130. Name the two foreigners who scored five of Southampton's goals in their 6-3 victory against Manchester United.

131. Which Dutch international scored a hat-trick against Wales in the 7-1 World Cup Qualifying win?

132. From which club did Southampton sign defender Ulrich Van Gobbel?

133. Name the former Inter Milan player who played for Sheffield Wednesday in 1996-97?

134. Tottenham added to their Scandanavian contingent when they signed who from Norwegian side Rosenberg in November '96?

135. How much did he cost?

121. **Alexei Mikhailichenko** 122. Patrick Vieira 123. **Kasey Keller** 124. Southampton 125. **Eyal Berkovic** 126. Savo Milosevic 127. **Georgios Donis** 128. Slaven Bilic 129. **Dani** 130. Egil Ostenstad and Eyal Berkovic 131. **Dennis Bergkamp** 132. Galatasaray 133. **Benito Carbone** 134. Stefan Iversen 135. **£2.7m**

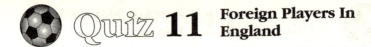

136. Name the Norwegian defender who has played for both Leeds and Oldham.

137. Which Ukrainian joined Coventry for a fee of £800,000 in January 1997?

138. Who did Middlesbrough sign from Inter Milan during 1996-97?

139. How much did Middlesbrough pay for him?

140. At the same time Middlesbrough signed a player from Slaven Bratislava. Who was he?

141. In February 1997, Blackburn signed a striker from Odense. Who?

142. Name the goalkeeper who left Bradford to join Middlesbrough.

143. Name the Dutch striker who joined Nottingham Forest for £4.5million in March '97.

144. From which club did he sign?

145. Name the two Costa Rican players who joined Derby in March '97.

146. Name the former Spurs striker who was part of Belgium's 1986 World Cup squad that finished fourth.

147. Name the Brazilian striker that Newcastle bought from Fluminense.

148. Name the Argentinian World Cup winner who had an FA Cup Final song named after him.

149. Which former Manchester United midfielder was part of the Danish World Cup side that reached the second round of the 1986 tournament?

150. Name the former Tottenham goalkeeper that played in the 1994 World Cup Finals for Norway.

151. Name the Arsenal player who became renowned for his poor goalscoring record.

152. From what club did he sign from?

153. Name the Estonian goalkeeper who joined Derby in 1997?

154. Which Premiership striker scored the winning goal that dented England's 1998 World Cup hopes?

155. Which two foreigners scored the goals against Stockport that effectively put Middlesbrough into the Coca-Cola Cup Final in 1997?

156. Name the Dutch defender that scored his first Premiership goal for Leeds v Everton in March 1997.

157. Name the Norwegian midfielder that joined Nottingham Forest in 1993.

158. Name the ex-Tottenham player that scored four goals for Romania in a World Cup qualifying game v Liechtenstein.

159. Which Finnish international had a spell at Bolton?

160. Who is the only foreigner to have captained a winning FA Cup Final side?

161. Who was the first foreigner to play in an FA Cup Final?

162. Which foreigner has made the most FA Cup Final appearances?

163. Name the two Belgium born players that played in FA Cup Finals during the 1980's.

164. Name the former Czeckoslovakian manager of Aston Villa.

165. From which club did Arsene Wenger leave to manage Arsenal?

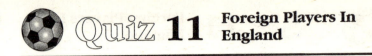
166. What nationality is Lionel Perez, Sunderland's goalkeeper in 1996-97?

167. Name Sunderland's Polish defender in the 1996-97 season.

168. Which Real Zaragoza player scored the wonder goal that defeated Arsenal in the 1994 Cup-Winners' Cup Final?

169. Which Premiership side did he previously play for?

170. Name the Portugese player who played for West Ham in 1996-97.

171. For which country does Georgiou Kinkladze play for?

172. From which club did Manchester City sign him from?

173. Although he has played for England, where was Matthew Le Tissier born?

174. Which Swedish international did Sheffield Wednesday buy from PSV Eindhoven for £2million in 1994?

175. Who did Liverpool sign from Rosenberg during the winter of 1996?

176. For which two Premiership clubs has Hans Segers played for?

177. In 1993 Sheffield United signed a Norwegian international for £400,000. Who was he?

178. Name the Bulgarian goalkeeper that appeared for Reading in the 96-97 season.

179. From which club did Arsenal sign French 17 year old Nicolas Anelka?

180. Who scored the winning goal for Tottenham in the 1981 FA Cup Final replay v Manchester City?

181. **Which Bulgarian played for Aberdeen in the 1996-97 season?**

182. Which Danish striker, who played in Euro '96, moved to Rangers in March 1996 for £1.5m?

183. **Who did Everton sell Andrei Kanchelskis to in 1997?**

184. Which World Cup goalscorer played for Rangers in the 1995-96 season?

185. **Which Danish striker was voted Scottish Player of the Year in 1995?**

186. Which German striker played for Celtic in the 1996-97 season?

187. **Can you name his Italian strike partner?**

188. Who was George Graham's last signing at Arsenal?

189. **Where did Graham sign him from?**

190. Who have Blackburn signed rom Halmstad?

191. **Who is the Dutchman who played for Derby in 1996-97?**

192. What nationality is Leicester's Pontus Kaamark?

193. **Who was W.B.A Canadian striker in the 1996-97 season?**

194. Which German defender played for Manchester City in the 1995-96 season?

195. **Which American goalkeeper has played in the Premiership for a London club?**

181. Ilian Kiriakov 182. Erik Bo Andersen 183. Fiorentina 184. Oleg Salenko 185. Brian Laudrup 186. Andreas Thom 187. Paulo Di Canio 188. Glenn Helder 189. Vitesse Arnhem 190. Niklas Gudmundsson 191. Robin Van der Laan 192. Swedish 193. Paul Peschisolido 194. Michael Frontzeck 195. Juergen Sommer

1. **AC Milan played in the 1993 World Club Cup, despite finishing runners-up in the European Cup. Why?**

2. Who were the first British club to play in the World Club Cup?

3. **Who scored the winning goal for Celtic in their first leg match against Racing Club of Argentina in 1967?**

4. Who didn't play in Celtic's away leg in 1967 after being hit by a stone in the pre-match warm-up?

5. **The 1967 match went to a replay after a 2-2 aggregate score. The replay was a brutal which Celtic lost 1-0. How many players were sent-off in the game?**

6. Who was the Manchester United player sent-off in the 1968 first leg against Estudiantes?

7. **What was the score in that game?**

8. Another United player was sent-off in the return leg at Old Trafford. Who?

9. **What was the score in the second leg between United and Estudiantes in 1968?**

10. Who scored United's goal?

11. **Which United player had a 'goal' disallowed in the final minute of the 1968 match?**

12. Who were the first British club to win the World Club Cup?

13. **Which Premiership manager played for Nottingham Forest in the 1980 Final against Nacional?**

14. Why did European Cup runners-up Malmo play in the 1979 Final?

15. **Where was the 1980 Final played?**

Tokyo

British club has won it **13. Martin O'Neill** 14. Forest declined to take part **15.**
No **12. Brian Kidd 11.** Willie Morgan 10. 1-1 **9.** George Best 8. **Estudiantes**
Celtic **3. Billy McNeill** 4. Ron Simpson **5.** Five 6. Nobby Stiles **7.** 1-0 to
1. Marseille were stripped of European Cup because of match-fixing 2.

16. Which famous Brazilian played for Flamenco against Liverpool in the 1981 Final?

17. **What was the score in the 1981 Final?**

18. Who was Liverpool's goalkeeper in that game?

19. **Two of Liverpool's players in the 1981 Final became management colleagues in 1997. Who are they?**

20. Kenny Dalglish played in the 1981 Final for Liverpool. Which other player in that game went on to become a manager at Anfield?

21. **Who did Aston Villa lose to in the 1983 Final?**

22. Which goalkeeper won one cap for England and played for Aston Villa in the 1981 Final?

23. **Liverpool did not take part in the 1977 Final against Boca Juniors. Who took their place?**

24. How many appearances have four-time European Champions, Liverpool, made in the World Club Cup?

25. **Which Argentinian played for Independiente against Liverpool in 1984 and later went on to score in the 1986 World Cup Final?**

26. Who were the last British side to compete in the World Club Cup?

27. **What year was it?**

28. Which Danish international played in Liverpool's 1984 defeat?

29. **Which former England striker played for Nottingham Forest in the 1980 Final?**

30. Which Aston Villa player played in the 1982 Final, and was still playing for the club in 1994?

Quiz 13 — International Questions

1. **What was the score between England and Germany when they met in America in 1993?**

2. Who scored for England in that game?

3. **Who was in goal for the disastrous 2-0 World Cup Qualifying defeat in Norway in 1992?**

4. Who scored a stunning free-kick for England against Holland at Wembley in the same year?

5. **Who got a brace of goals for England against Turkey in 1992?**

6. What was the score in England's friendly against Brazil in May 1992?

7. **Which two England players made their full international debuts in the 1-0 win in Hungary in 1991?**

8. Which striker scored on his England debut against France in Feburary 1992?

9. **Who were England's opponents at Wembley in September 1991 for the first defeat of Graham Taylors's reign?**

10. Who made his England debut against USSR in May 1991 as a substitute?

11. **Who returned to the England side for the European Championship Qualifier against Ireland in Dublin in 1990?**

12. Which North African country did England play in their last friendly prior to the 1990 World Cup?

13. **Who defeated England at Wembley in May 1990?**

14. Who scored twice against Czechoslovakia in March 1990 at Wembley?

15. **Who scored for England against Yugoslavia at Wembley earlier that same year?**

1. **2-1 to Germany** 2. David Platt 3. **Chris Woods** 4. John Barnes 5. **Paul Gascoigne** 6. 1-1 7. **Nigel Martyn and Keith Curle** 8. Alan Shearer 9. **Germany** 10. David Batty 11. **Gordon Cowans** 12. Tunisia 13. **Uruguay** 14. Steve Bull 15. **Bryan Robson**

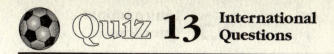

16. Who were England's opponents for three successive goalless draws in 1989?

17. **Who came on to score on his England debut at Hampden Park in 1989?**

18. Which Middle Eastern country gained a 1-1 draw with England in 1988?

19. **Who did Paul Gascoigne make his England debut against?**

20. Which South American country drew 1-1 with England in May 1988?

21. **Who were beaten 8-0 at Wembley in October 1987?**

22. Which Premiership manager made his last full international appearance against West Germany in September 1987?

23. **Who scored all four goals in England's win over Spain in Madrid in 1987?**

24. Which nation beat England 1-0 in September 1987?

25. **Who scored two goals in England's win over Mexico in a friendly prior to the 1986 World Cup Finals?**

26. Which current manager ended his international career against Scotland at Wembley in 1986?

27. **Who scored in England's 3-0 win over West Germany in 1985?**

28. Who did Gary Lineker score his first international goal against?

29. **Which goalkeeper made his debut in that same game?**

30. Which two players shared the goals in England's 4-1 win over Finland in 1982?

16. Sweden, Poland and Italy 17. **Steve Bull** 19. **Denmark** 20. Colombia 21. **Turkey** 22. Peter Reid 23. **Gary Lineker** 24. Sweden 25. **Mark Hateley** 26. Trevor Francis 27. **Kerry Dixon (2) and Bryan Robson** 28. Republic of Ireland 29. **Gary Bailey** 30. Bryan Robson and Paul Mariner.

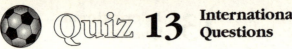
31. **Which former West Ham winger made his only two England appearances in 1982?**

32. Against whom did Bryan Robson make his England debut in 1980?

33. **Which side crushed England 4-1 in the 1979/80 season?**

34. Who scored for England in the 4-3 defeat in Austria in 1979?

35. **Who scored the England goals in the 2-0 win over Italy at Wembley in 1977?**

36. Which player scored for England against Finland in October 1976?

37. **What was the score when England beat Scotland in May 1975?**

38. Which country were beaten 7-0 by England at Wembley in 1973?

39. **Which country became the first to win at Wembley in six years when they won 3-1 in a European Championship Qualifier in April 1972?**

40. Who were beaten 6-1 by England in a 1966 World Cup warm up game?

41. **Who scored four goals in that game?**

42. Who beat England 5-1 in 1964?

43. **Who did England beat 10-0 in 1964?**

44. Which players scored four and three goals respectively in that game?

45. **Who left Wembley in 1963 having been thrashed 8-3?**

46. Jimmy Greaves scored four goals in that game but who notched a hat-trick?

47. Which side did England also put eight past in that same year?

48. Which goalkeeper conceded five in a European Championship Qualifier in Paris in 1963?

49. Who scored in the famous 9-3 Wembley win over Scotland in 1961?

50. Who did England also score nine and eight goals respectively against that year?

51. Which side beat England 5-0 in a warm up game for the 1958 World Cup finals?

52. In what year did Bobby Charlton make his England debut?

53. Which former England coach also played in that game?

54. Against which South American country did Bobby Moore make his debut?

55. Which home nation were beaten 10-0 by England on their ground in 1947?

56. Who did England lose to in the first friendly after the disastrous 1992 European Championship?

57. What was the score when England beat a Milla-less Cameroon at Wembley in Feburary 1991?

58. How many goals did England manage during three friendlies with Australia in June 1983?

59. Which country beat England 4-1 in May 1959?

60. Who did England play in their first game after the 1966 World Cup?

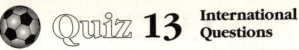

61. **What was the score in the famous England-Hungary game at Wembley in 1953?**

62. In the return game in Budapest the following year how many goals did Hungary put past the hapless England defence?

63. **Which former England manager scored twice in the 5-1 win in Denmark in 1955?**

64. Who was the first substitute to be used by England?

65. **Who were the only country to keep a clean sheet against England between May 1955 and May 1958?**

66. Which England player grabbed four goals in the 7-2 win over Scotland in April 1955?

67. **Who scored for England in the 3-1 win over West Germany in Berlin in 1956?**

68. Which players scored twice in England's 7-0 rout of Austria in 1973?

69. **Which England player scored twice in the 5-1 win over Scotland in 1975?**

70. Who scored the only goal in Budapest in May 1992?

71. **Which player scored on his debut in the World Cup Qualifier in Turkey in May 1991?**

72. Who played in goal for England against Brazil in 1978?

73. **Who scored twice for England in the 3-0 win over Czechoslovakia in 1974?**

74. Which Chairman scored in the 1-1 draw with Wales in April 1970?

75. **Against which nation did Peter Shilton make his England debut?**

76. Which country defeated England 1-0 at Wembley in May 1972?

77. **Which England players scored twice in the 5-2 win over Belguim in 1947?**

78. Who scored four goals for England in the 9-2 victory over Northern Ireland in 1949?

79. **Which England midfielder scored twice in the 4-0 win at home to Norway in September 1980?**

80. Who came on as a substitute to grab the equaliser away to lowly Iceland in his only England appearance in June 1982?

81. **Who scored twice for England in the impressive 3-1 win over World Champions Argentina in May 1980?**

82. Who plundered all five England goals in the win over Cyprus in April 1975?

83. **Who scored the goals in the 2-2 draw with Argentina in May 1974?**

84. From which Scandanavian country did England beat 5-1 in 1956?

85. **Which England defender made his debut in the 1-0 win away to Holland in 1969?**

86. Who scored the only goal of that game?

87. **Which former Ipswich player scored his only England goal in the 5-1 win over Scotland in 1975?**

88. Which ground staged England's 1995 Umbro Cup match against Sweden?

89. **Who scored his first England goal in that game?**

90. Which country conceded five goals at Wembley in May 1994?

76. Northern Ireland 77. **Tommy Lawton and Tom Finney** 78. John Rowley 79. **Terry McDermott** 80. Paul Goddard 81. **David Johnson** 82. Malcolm MacDonald 83. **Mike Channon and Frank Worthington** 84. Finland 85. **Emlyn Hughes** 86. Colin Bell 87. **Kevin Beattie** 88. Elland Road, Leeds 89. **Teddy Sheringham** 90. Greece

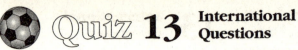

91. Which nation defeated Scotland at Hampden in March 1994?

92. Who scored the goals in Scotland's 2-1 win against Austria in April 1994?

93. Who scored the Scottish goal in the 1-1 draw with Switzerland in the World Cup Qualifier in September 1993?

94. Which Premiership player grabbed the consolation goal in Scotland's 3-1 defeat in Rome the following month?

95. Which country did Scotland beat 6-1 in September 1984?

96. Which East European country did Scotland beat in Glasgow in March 1986?

97. Which nation did Scotland beat 7-2 in 1929?

98. Which Middle Eastern country embarrassed Scotland 3-1 in their only ever meeting, at Hampden in 1990?

99. What was the score in the inaugural game with the 'Auld Enemy'?

100. Who scored for Scotland in the 1-1 draw with Russia at Hampden in 1994?

101. Against which country did Denis Law make his Scottish debut?

102. Who scored Scotland's winnner against England in November 1964?

103. Who scored Scotland's goal against Spain in Valencia in 1975?

104. Which striker scored the Scotland goal in the draw with Belguim in 1983?

105. Where did Wales and Scotland meet in their 1977 World Cup Play-Off game?

105. Anfield

91. Holland 92. Tosh McKinlay and Billy McGinlay **93. John Collins** 94. Kevin Gallacher **95. Yugoslavia** 96. Romania **97. Norway** 98. Egypt **99. 0-0** 100. Scott Booth **101. Holland** 102. Alan Gilzean **103. Joe Jordan** 104. Charlie Nicholas

106. What was the result of that game?

107. Who scored a hat-trick for Wales in their 1957 World Cup Qualifier against East Germany?

108. Which country beat Northern Ireland 8-2 in the 1950 British Championship?

109. Which nation beat Northern Ireland for qualification to the 1978 World Cup Finals?

110. Which two countries did Northern Irleand beat in that group?

111. Who is Northern Ireland's most capped player?

112. Which Republic of Ireland player was sent-off against Macedonia in a 1998 World Cup qualifyer?

113. Name the three England players of the early 1990's who started their careers at Crewe?

114. Which striker won two caps for England, but played only 18 minutes?

115. Which England international was once loaned out to Aldershot early in his career?

116. Who was the last British player to be voted European Footballer of the Year?

117. When Matthias Sammer made his debut for Germany, it was his 24th cap. How come?

118. Who, in 1993, became the first black player to captain England?

119. In one of soccer's biggest tragedy's which national team was killed in a plane crash en-route to a 1993 World Cup quali-fyer?

120. Who was named new England captain after Euro 96?

1. Who scored Rangers' winning goal in the 1971 Scottish League Cup Final?

2. What was the score recorded in the 1984 Scottish Cup, which remains a British record this century?

3. Who was Scotland's Player of the Year in 1996?

4. Which team beat Celtic 3-1 in the 1970 Scottish Cup Final?

5. Which Scottish club signed Norwich City's Kevin Drinkell for £500,000 at the start of the 1987-88 season?

6. Who was voted Scotland's Young Player of the Year in 1981?

7. Which two teams shared the Division One title in the first season in 1891?

8. Who won the first Scottish Premier Division in 1976?

9. Who was voted Player of the Year by the Scottish Football Writers in 1974?

10. Which former Chelsea star was voted Second Division Player of the Year by the SFA in 1982?

11. Which Dutchman was voted Premier Division Player of the Year by the SFA in 1989?

12. Who was the first player since 1972 to score a hat-trick in the Scottish FA Cup Final in 1996?

13. Where were both Scottish FA Cup semi-finals played in 1996?

14. Who did Celtic beat in the 1995 Scottish FA Cup Final?

15. Who won six of the first nine Scottish FA Cup Finals?

1. **Derek Johnstone** 2. Stirling Albion 20 Selkirk 0 in 1984 3. **Paul Gascoigne** 4. Aberdeen 5. **Rangers** 6. Charlie Nicholas 7. **Dumbarton and Rangers** 8. Rangers 9. **The Scotland World Cup Squad** 10. Pat Nevin 11. **Theo Snelders** 12. Gordon Durie 13. **Hampden Park** 14. Airdrieonians 15. **Queen's Park**

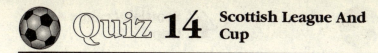

16. When was the first Rangers-Celtic Scottish FA Cup Final?

17. **Who won?**

18. Why was the FA Cup withheld in 1909?

19. **Which team won the FA Cup four times in five seasons in the early 1980's?**

20. Who was voted Scottish Manager of the Year in 1990?

21. **Before the end of the 1996-97 season, who was the last Scottish player to be voted Player of the Year by the SFA?**

22. What year was it?

23. **What was the highest score in the Scottish FA Cup, and still a British record?**

24. What year was it in?

25. **On that same day Dundee Harp beat which team 35-0 in the Cup?**

26. 11 goals were scored in the Premier Division game between Celtic and Hamilton in January 1987. What was the score-line?

27. **How many goals did Celtic score when the two teams met again in November 1988?**

28. Which Scottish team holds the British record score this century?

29. **Nine players scored that day. Which player got seven goals?**

30. Which Dundee United striker scored five times in the Premier Division against Morton in November 1984?

31. **Which Ayr player set a British record of 66 League goals in one season in 1927-28?**

32. When Arbroath beat Bon Accord in the 1885 Scottish Cup, how many goals did John Petrie score?

33. **Who is the Scottish League's top scorer with 410 goals?**

34. Which player scored 338 League goals in a career that started at St Mirren and finished at Clapton Orient?

35. **Which club did Gerry Baker score 10 goals against for St Mirren in the 1960 Scottish Cup first round?**

36. Which team scored 142 goals in just 34 League games in the 1937-38 season?

37. **Which team conceded just 19 goals in 36 Premier Division games in 1990?**

38. Who scored the fastest goal in Scottish Cup history for Aberdeen in 1982?

39. **How many seconds was it?**

40. Which former Motherwell striker, later to play for Liverpool, scored the fastest hat-trick in Scottish history in 1959?

41. **Which Scottish goalkeeper scored for Hibernian in 1988?**

42. Who did he score against?

43. **Which other goalkeeper has scored in a League match?**

44. Which Danish striker scored in 15 consecutive matches for Dundee United in 1964-65?

45. **Which Scottish club went 14 consecutive games without scoring to set a British record?**

46. Which two Scottish teams attracted an attendance of 143,470 in March 1948?

47. **How many people were inside Hampden Park for the 1937 Scottish Cup Final?**

48. 135,826 turned up to watch Celtic play an European Cup semi-final in 1970. Which other British team were they playing?

49. **What is the record attendance for a Scottish League Cup Final?**

50. Which two teams were playing?

51. **Who captained Aberdeen to Scottish Cup glory in 1970, and then led Manchester United to FA Cup glory seven years later?**

52. Four players were sent-off when Rangers faced Celtic in the Scottish Cup quarter-final in 1991. Can you name the players?

53. **Which former Scottish international was sent-off 11 times in Scottish matches?**

54. How many times was he sent-off for Scotland?

55. **Which two Hearts players were suspended by the Scottish FA for fighting each other in a 'friendly' game?**

56. Billy McLafferty was banned for eight-and-a-half months and fined £250 by the Scottish FA. Why?

57. **Which club was he playing for at the time?**

58. Which former Rangers striker was banned for 12 games for violent conduct in a game against Raith in 1994?

59. **Which manager was also chairman of the club at the same time, in 1988?**

60. Which club was he at?

46. Rangers and Hibernian 47. 146,433 48. Leeds 49. 107,609 50. Celtic and Rangers 51. **Martin Buchan** 52. Terry Hurlock, Mark Walters and Mark Hateley of Rangers and Peter Grant of Celtic 53. **Willie Johnston** 54. Once 55. **Graeme Hogg and Craig Levein** 56. Because he had failed to turn up to a disciplinary hearing after being sent-off 57. **Stenhousemuir** 58. Duncan Ferguson 59. **Jim McLean** 60. Dundee United

61. **66 people died when they were trampled near the end of the Rangers-Celtic match in 1971. Where did the tragedy happen**

62. Which Celtic goalkeeper died after suffering a fractured skull against Rangers in 1931?

63. **How was the 1987 Scottish League Cup Final decided?**

64. Who won the game?

65. **What was the penalty shoot-out score between Aberdeen and Celtic in the 1990 Scottish Cup Final?**

66. Celtic lost the Scottish League Cup Final on penalties. To which side?

67. **Which team won every match in the Scottish League in the 1898-99 season?**

68. Before the 1997-98 season, how many times have Rangers completed the League and Cup double?

69. **Before the 1997-98 season, how many times have Rangers completed the domestic treble?**

70. How many trophies did Celtic win in the 1966-67 season?

71. **Who were the last club to win the Scottish Cup for three years in succession?**

72. When was that?

73. **Before the 1997 Final, who are the three players to be sent-off in Scottish Cup Finals?**

74. Who holds the record for unbeaten matches in the Scottish League?

75. **How many games were they unbeaten?**

61. **Rangers' Ibrox Park** 62. John Thomson 63. **Penalties** 64. Rangers, beating Aberdeen 65. **9-8 to Aberdeen** 66. Raith Rovers 67. **Rangers** 68. 14 69. **Five** 70. Five 71. **Aberdeen** 72. 1982-83-84 73. **Jock Buchanan, Roy Aitken and Walter Kidd** 74. Celtic 75. **62 matches**

76. Who became the first player to score 200 goals in the Premier Division?

77. **Which team set a Scottish League record of 40 consecutive home defeats in the 1990's?**

78. Which team collected a total of 67 points out of a possible 72 in the 1963-64 season?

79. **Which Rangers player won nine Scottish Championship medals in 11 years?**

80. Who were the first Scottish club to play in the European Cup?

81. **What season was it?**

82. Which round did they reach?

83. **What season was the first Premier Division played?**

84. Who were the sponsors of the 1996-97 Scottish FA Cup?

85. **What year did the Scottish FA introduce penalty shoot-outs to the Cup Final?**

86. Who provided the shock of the 1995 Scottish Cup by beating Aberdeen 2-0?

87. **Who did Tommy Burns leave to become manager of Celtic?**

88. Which manager was fined £2,000 by the SFA for breach of contract?

89. **When was the Scottish FA formed?**

90. Who became the youngest player in the Scottish League when he played for Queen's Park in 1946?

76. Ally McCoist 77. **Cowdenbeath** 78. Greenock Morton 79. **Alan Morton** 80. Hibernian 81. 1955-56 82. The semi-final 83. 1975-76 84. Tennents 85. 1990 86. Stenhousemuir 87. **Kilmarnock** 88. Tommy Burns 89. 1873 90. Ronnie Simpson

Quiz 14 Scottish League And Cup

91. How old was he?

92. Who remains the oldest player to earn his first cap for Scotland?

93. How old was he - and who did he play against?

94. Which two Scottish sides shared Firhill Park for five years?

95. Which Scottish club play their home games at Hampden Park?

96. Who were the first Scottish club to have an artificial pitch?

97. Which goalkeeper played for Scotland Under-21's in the afternoon and then turned out for Clyde that same evening?

98. Who were the first Scottish club to issue a Stock Exchange share issue?

99. Which two Scottish clubs have won the European Cup-Winners Cup?

100. Which Scottish club beat Eintracht Frankfurt 5-1 in an Uefa Cup first round, second leg, after losing the first leg 3-0?

101. Which clubs did Alex Ferguson play for?

102. How many Scottish League clubs did Alex Ferguson manage before joining Manchester United?

103. Name them.

104. Who was named Scottish Manager of the Year in 1995?

105. Which goalkeeper was named 1981 Player of the Year?

91. 15 92. Ronnie Simpson 93. against England 94. Partick Thistle and Clyde 95. Queen's Park 96. Stirling Albion 97. Scott Howie 98. Hibernian 99. Rangers and Aberdeen 100. Kilmarnock 101. Queen's Park, St Johnstone, Dunfermline, Rangers, Falkirk and Ayr United 102. Three 103. East Stirling, St Mirren and Aberdeen 104. Jimmy Nicholl (Raith) 105. Alan Rough

1. **How many times have Moyola Park won the Irish F. A. Cup?**

2. Who were the Irish League champions in 1982?

3. **In the 1995-96 Irish Premier Division, who finished higher, Glenavon or Glentoran?**

4. Waterford were FAI League Champions for three consecutive seasons. Name the years.

5. **Who was the 1996 Irish Premier Division Player of the Year?**

6. Name the 1996 Smirnoff Irish Premier Division Manager of the Year.

7. **In the replay of the 1996 FAI Cup Final, how many players with the surname Geoghegan played in the Shelbourne side?**

8. Which club were relegated from the Irish Premier Division at the end of the 1995 - 96 season?

9. **In the 1995-96 FAI Premier Division, which club had three points deducted for fielding players deemed to be 'illegal' ?**

10. Who scored the winning goal for Glentoran in last year's Irish Cup Final?

11. **The 1996 Bord Gais FAI League Cup Final between Shelbourne and Sligo Rovers was decided on penalties. Who won and what was the score?**

12. Who were the Irish League Champions in 1976?

13. **How many times have Shamrock Rovers completed the FAI League and Cup double ?**

14. Who was the 1995-96 FAI Premier Division's Young Player of the Year?

15. **Who was the 1995-96 Irish Premier Division's top scorer?**

Quiz 16 Welsh League And Cup

1. **Which team beat Barry Town on penalties to win the 1996 Welsh Cup?**

2. Who won the first Welsh Cup?

3. **Who did they beat in the Final?**

4. Which team won the Welsh Cup for five consecutive years from 1967?

5. **Who did Cardiff City lose the Cup Final to in 1939?**

6. Which team appeared in the Cup Final on six occasions in eight years from 1887?

7. **When was the last time Aberwystwyth won the Welsh Cup?**

8. Which non-league team did Cardiff City beat in the 1992 Cup Final?

9. **Cardiff City played in 11 consecutive Cup Finals from 1967. True or False?**

10. Who were the Welsh League Champions in 1995?

11. **Who did Swansea beat 8-0 in the Welsh Cup quarter-finals in 1995?**

12. Bangor City won 12-1 in the fourth round of the 1995 Welsh Cup fourth round. Who were their victims?

13. **Shrewsbury lost the 1931 Cup Final 7-0. To who?**

14. Which famous non-league side reached the Cup Final twice in the 1980's?

15. **Who were the first club to win the Welsh Cup in a penalty shoot-out?**

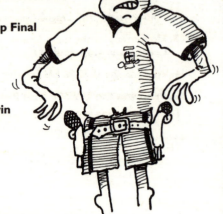

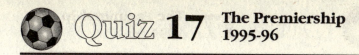

1. **Who broke his leg in the 1-1 draw between Blackburn and Middlesbrough in December?**

2. Who scored after just 12 seconds against Coventry in September 1995?

3. **Who became the youngest Premiership player when he turned out for West Ham at Manchester City on New Year's Day in 1996?**

4. Who scored a hat-trick on the opening day of the season but was still on the losing side?

5. **Who scored Manchester United's consolation goal in a 3-1 defeat at Aston Villa on the opening day of the season?**

6. Why did Manchester United change their grey away kit at half-time at Southampton in the 1995-96 season?

7. **Who scored Leeds' two goals in their win at West Ham?**

8. Who was sent-off for West Ham at Manchester United in 1995-96?

9. **Who scored three goals in the first three games for Manchester United in the 1995-96 season?**

10. Defending champions, Blackburn, lost three of their first four games of the season. Which clubs beat them?

11. **Which former Everton players scored for the club against Southampton in 1995-96?**

12. Which striker scored against his former club for Nottingham Forest in a 1-1 draw in August?

13. **Which two foreign players scored for Coventry in a 2-2 draw at Chelsea in the 1995-96 season?**

14. Which Belgian international scored for Sheffield Wednesday at Wimbledon?

15. **Which veteran striker scored the only goal for Wimbledon against Liverpool in September?**

1. **Graeme Le Saux** 2. Aston Villa's Dwight Yorke 3. **West Ham's Neil Finn (17 years, 3 days)** 4. (**3 days**) 5. Matthew Le Tissier 6. The players complained that they couldn't see each other 7. **Tony Yeboah** 8. Marco Boogers 9. **Roy Keane** 10. Sheffield Wednesday, Bolton and Manchester United 11. **Anders Limpar and Daniel Amokachi** 12. Kevin Campbell 13. **Marques Isaias and Peter Ndlovu** 14. Marc Degryse 15. **Mick Harford**

16. Which three England internationals scored for Liverpool in their 3-0 win against Blackburn in September 1995?

17. **Who scored his first two goals for Arsenal in a 4-2 win against Southampton?**

18. Robbie Fowler scored four times against Bolton in a 5-2 victory but who scored the other Liverpool goal?

19. **Who crowned his Middlesbrough debut with a goal in the opening day draw at Arsenal?**

20. Eric Cantona capped his return from suspension to score from the penalty spot to equalise for Manchester United in the 2-2 draw against Liverpool. Who scored United's first goal?

21. **Who scored for Chelsea against his former club but lost the match 4-1 in October?**

22. Chris Armstrong scored his first goal for Tottenham against which club?

23. **What was the scoreline when Manchester City played at Liverpool in October?**

24. Manchester City won their first league of the season against Bolton. But what month was it in?

25. **Who beat Nottingham Forest 7-0 in November?**

26. Who scored both Everton goals in the Merseyside derby at Anfield?

27. **Manchester United scored three goals in the first eight minutes in a 4-1 win in November. Against which team?**

28. Who won the North London derby at White Hart Lane?

29. **Who scored a hat-trick but was on the losing side against Shefield Wednesday in December?**

30. Blackburn were beaten 5-0 in December. By who?

31. **Who was sent-off for West Ham in their 3-0 defeat at Everton in December?**

32. Who was beaten 6-2 by Sheffield Wednesday in December?

33. **Which player scored five goals in two games against Coventry in the 1995-96 season?**

34. Who scored all four goals for Liverpool when they twice met Manchester United in the season?

35. **Which former Tottenham player scored against his old club in Bolton's 2-2 draw in December?**

36. Who did Leeds beat 3-1 on Christmas Eve?

37. **Who was sent-off in Wimbledon's 2-1 defeat of Chelsea on Boxing Day?**

38. Which two England internationals scored two of the four goals that Tottenham put past Manchester United on New Year's day?

39. **Who scored an injury time winner for Chelsea against QPR in January?**

40. Which two players scored twice when Liverpool beat Leeds 5-0 at Anfield in January?

41. **Who scored Manchester United's only goal in their win at West Ham?**

42. Who scored a hat-trick for Chelsea in a 5-0 victory against Middlesbrough in February?

43. **Which foreign star won the Tottenham-West Ham match with a goal after five minutes?**

44. Who won 4-1 at Middlesbrough in February?

45. **How many goals did Manchester United put past Bolton when they met in February?**

31. **Ludek Miklosko** 32. Leeds 33. **Savo Milosevic** 34. Robbie Fowler 35. **Gudni Bergsson** 36. Manchester United 37. **Vinnie Jones** 38. Teddy Sheringham, Sol Campbell 39. **Paul Furlong** 40. Neil Ruddock and Robbie Fowler 41. Eric Cantona 42. Gavin Peacock 43. **Dani** 44. Bolton 45. **Six**

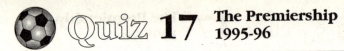

46. Which two Chelsea players scored when they met Wimbledon in March?

47. **Which team scored three goals in eight minutes against Aston Villa in March?**

48. Who scored twice for Arsenal in their 3-1 victory over Manchester City in March?

49. **Which Dutch international scored both goals in Sheffield Wednesday's 3-2 defeat at Aston Villa?**

50. 50,028 watched the Manchester United-Arsenal match in March. What was the score?

51. **Arsenal beat Newcastle 2-0 in March. Which Scottish defender scored the first goal?**

52. The 4-3 win for Liverpool against Newcastle was dubbed "game of the decade". Who scored Newcastle's three goals?

53. **Who scored the winner in the Manchester derby in April?**

54. Which striker scored twice to help Blackburn beat Newcastle at Ewood Park?

55. **Who scored his first hat-trick for Chelsea in the 4-1 victory over Leeds in April?**

56. Blackburn's 5-1 win at Nottingham Forest included two goals from an England international. Who was it?

57. **Who scored Manchester United's consolation in their 3-1 defeat at Southampton?**

58. What was the result at Goodison Park in the Merseyside derby?

59. **Who scored a hat-trick for Everton in their 5-2 win at Sheffield Wednesday in April?**

60. When Manchester United beat Nottingham Forest 5-0 who scored twice?

46. **Paul Furlong and a Steve Clarke own goal 47. Liverpool** 48. John Harrson 49. **Regi Blinker** 50. 1-0 to United 51. **Scott Marshall** 52. Les Ferdinand, David Ginola and Faustino Asprilla 53. **Ryan Giggs of United** 54. Graham Fenton 55. **Mark Hughes** 56. Jason Wilcox 57. **Ryan Giggs** 58. 1-1 59. **Andrei Kanchelskis** 60. David Beckham

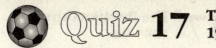

61. Who scored Newcastle's only goal in a 1-0 win at Leeds?

62. Which England international scored twice at Elland Road in Tottenham's 3-1 win in May?

63. Which two internationals scored in the last ten minutes to give Arsenal a 2-1 win over Bolton on the last day of the season?

64. Who scored a goal on his last appearance for the club when Manchester City and Liverpool drew on the final day of the season?

65. Manchester United won the Premiership title with a 3-0 win at Middlesbrough. Who scored their goals?

66. Which team beat West Ham 3-0 but ended the day relegated?

67. Which team claimed the last Uefa Cup on the final day of the season?

68. Which two teams both had goalless draws on the last day of the season to stave off relegation?

69. Which German made his debut for Manchester City in the opening day draw against Tottenham?

70. Who scored the Goal of the Season?

71. Who scored three goals in the first two games of the season for his new club?

72. Who scored and was later sent-off in Wimbledon's 3-0 win at QPR in August?

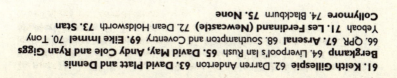

73. Who scored the only goal of the game on his debut for Liverpool against Sheffield Wednesday?

74. Who did Bolton beat for their first win in the Premiership?

75. Andrea Silenzi became the first Italian to play in the Premiership when he joined Nottingham Forest. How many league goals did he score in his first season?

Collymore 74. Blackburn 75. None
Yeboah 71. Les Ferdinand (Newcastle) 72. Dean Holdsworth 73. Stan
66. QPR 67. Arsenal 68. Southampton and Coventry 69. Eike Immel 70. Tony
Bergkamp 64. Liverpool's Ian Rush 65. David May, Andy Cole and Ryan Giggs
61. Keith Gillespie 62. Darren Anderton 63. David Platt and Dennis

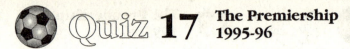
76. Which Wimbledon player thought he had been sent-off against Liverpool, instead of Vinnie Jones?

77. Who had his sending-off revolked in September?

78. Who scored twice for QPR in a 3-1 win at Leeds in September?

79. Who made his Liverpool debut against Blackburn in September?

80. Who was sent-off for West Ham at Arsenal in September?

81. Who scored against his former club for Newcastle in a 3-2 win in October?

82. Who scored on his debut for Blackburn in a 2-1 win over Southampton in October?

83. Who earned a three-match suspension after stamping on Chelsea's John Spencer's head?

84. Who replaced sent-off Paul Heald as Wimbledon goalkeeper when they lost 6-1 at Newcastle?

85. Who scored a last-minute winner for Newcastle over Liverpool in November?

86. Who made his debut for Middlesbrough in their 1-1 draw against Leeds in November?

87. Who lost their record 25-game unbeaten run with a 7-0 defeat at Blackburn?

88. Who scored a superb goal for Bolton in their 3-2 defeat at Chelsea in November?

89. Who made his Premiership debut at the age of 34 for QPR in December?

90. Which England player was sent-off for Arsenal at Southampton in December?

1. **The United States finished in third place in which World Cup?**

2. Who failed a routine drugs test in the 1994 World Cup and as a result was expelled from the competition?

3. **This Colombian player scored an own goal when playing the United States in the 1994 World Cup. What was his name and what happened when he returned home?**

4. Which two past winners failed to qualify for the 1994 World Cup finals?

5. **Name the three countries to make their World Cup debut in the 1994 finals?**

6. Who was Brazil's captain in the 1970 World Cup?

7. **Which manager recieved a one-match touchline ban and a £10,000 fine from FIFA in the 1994 finals?**

8. In the World Cup campaigns of 1990 and 1994 Ireland have played nine games. How many did they actually win?

9. **The United States played Brazil in the second round of the 1994 World Cup. What was the score?**

10. Who beat USA 7-1 in the 1934 World Cup?

11. **Wales missed out on qualifying for the 1994 World Cup. Who was their manager at the time?**

12. Altogether there were 52 games played in the 1990 World Cup. How many players were sent off?

13. **Which captain has led two losing teams in the World Cup finals?**

14. Which team beat the defending champions Argentina in the opening match of the 1990 World Cup finals?

15. **Who was the top goalscorer of the 1990 World Cup?**

1. **1930 World Cup - Uruguay** 2. Diego Maradona 3. **Andres Escobar** 4. Uruguay and England 5. **Saudi Arabia, Greece and Nigeria** 6. Carlos Alberto 7. **Jack Charlton** 8. Two 9. **Brazil won 1-0** 10. Italy 11. **Terry Yorath** 12. 16 13. **Karl-Heinz Rummenigge** 14. Cameroon 15. Salvatore Schillaci

16. Who was Cameroon's famous centre-forward in the 1990 finals?

17. **West Germany beat Holland 2-1 in the second round of the 1990 finals. During the game which Dutch player was sent off for spitting?**

18. Dutch manager Leo Beenhakker went on to manage which international team in the 1994 World Cup?

19. **In the 1990 World Cup who won the Fair Play award?**

20. Who became the first man to captain and manage a World Cup winning side?

21. **How many players were there left on the pitch at the end of the 1990 World Cup final?**

22. In 1990 Scotland qualified but once again failed to get past the first phase. How many times had this happened before?

23. **What nationality was the referee in the England v Argentina 'Hand of God' 1986 quarter-final?**

24. Ray Wilkins was sent off when England played Morocco in their second game of the 1986 finals. What for?

25. **Who returned from a two-year suspension to become the top goalscorer in the 1982 World Cup?**

26. In the 1982 semi-final West German keeper Harald Schumacher knocked unconscious which French defender in a now infamous challenge?

27. **After this incident what action did the referee take?**

28. Two Ipswich Town players played a major role in the English 1982 World Cup team. Who were they?

29. **Who captained the French team in the 1982 finals?**

30. How many games did England lose before being eliminated from the 1982 World Cup?

16. Roger Milla 17. **Frank Rijkaard** 18. Saudi Arabia 19. **England** 20. Franz Beckenbauer 21. **20** 22. 7 23. **Tunisian** 24. For throwing the ball at the referee 25. **Paulo Rossi** 26. Patrick Battiston 27. **He awarded West Germany a goal kick** 28. Mick Mills and Paul Mariner 29. **Michel Platini - check** 30. None

31. How many goals did England conceed before being eliminated from the 1982 World Cup?

32. Northern Ireland progressed to the second phase of the 1982 World Cup. When were the other occasions they have for the finals?

33. Argentina had to beat Peru by four goals to reach the 1978 World Cup final, they won 6-0. Where was the Peruvian goalkeeper Quiroga born?

34. Which Scottish player failed a random drugs test in the 1978 finals and was sent home?

35. What was used for the first time in the 1974 World Cup finals?

36. Which player has appeared in five World Cup tournaments?

37. The fastest goal in a World Cup final was scored by who in 1974?

38. England failed to qualify in 1974 thanks to which team?

39. Name the Dutch captain for the 1974 finals?

40. Who was the top goalscorer in the 1970 World Cup?

41. England, Wales, Scotland and Northern Ireland were not eligible to participate in the first World Cup in Uruguay 1930 - why?

42. England made their World Cup debut in which tournament?

43. In the 1950 World Cup England lost 1-0 to a team of rank outsiders, who were they?

44. What did Brazil get to keep after winning the 1970 World Cup?

45. Who scored the only, goal of the 1990 World Cup final?

31. One 32. 1958 and 1986 33. Argentina 34. Willie Johnstone 35. A new trophy. The FIFA World Cup replaced the old Jules Rimet trophy. 36. The Mexican goalkeeper Antonio Carbajal who appeared in the 1950 World Cup through to the 1966 World Cup. 37. Johan Neeskens 38. Poland 39. Johan Cruyff 40. Gerhard Muller 41. They had withdrawn from FIFA in 1928 42. Brazil in 1950 43. USA 44. Jules Rimet trophy 45. Andreas Brehme

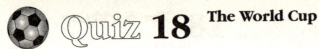

46. Who refused to shake hands with the President of FIFA after the 1990 World Cup final?

47. Which team did Alf Ramsey brand "animals" in the 1966 World Cup?

48. Who scored England's two goals against Portugal in the 1966 World Cup semi-final?

49. Which country has withdrawn from the World Cup on four occasions?

50. In 1966 which team were pelted with rotten fruit on their return from England?

51. What was the name of the dog who found the stolen Jules Rimet trophy in 1966?

52. Who was captain of the England 1962 World Cup team?

53. How old was Pele when he made his World Cup debut for Brazil in 1958?

54. Who was the first person to score a goal in the World Cup finals?

55. What was stolen from the Olympic Stadium in Rome on 8 July after the 1990 World Cup?

56. What was the name of the Italian 1990 World Cup mascot?

57. What fruit was the 1982 Spanish World Cup mascot based on?

58. In 1974 West Germany had two children as their World Cup mascots. What were their names?

59. How many times has the host nation won the World Cup?

60. Why did Uruguay refuse to defend their World Cup title in Italy in 1934?

46. Diego Maradona 47. **Argentina** 48. Bobby Charlton 49. **Egypt withdrew in 1938, 1958, 1962 and 1966.** 50. Italy – North Korea knocked them out. 51. **Pickles** 52. Johnny Haynes 53. **17** 54. Louis Laurent of France 55. **The reinforced centre spot** 56. Ciao 57. **Orange** 58. Tip and Tap 59. **Five** 60. Because so few European countries participated in their World Cup in 1930.

61. Which team has held the World Cup the longest?

62. In which World Cup was Britain represented by all four Home Countries?

63. Who were the first country to hold both the European Championship and the World Cup at the same time?

64. What has been the highest score in a World Cup finals match?

65. Who holds the individual goal scoring record in a World Cup tournament?

66. Who was the manager of the 1974 Dutch World Cup squad?

67. The 1986 World Cup final was held in which stadium?

68. Who won the Most Exciting Team award at the 1994 World Cup?

69. Who won the Fair Play award at the 1994 World Cup?

70. Which two ex-England players recently backed Japan's failed bid for the 2002 World Cup?

71. How many countries will be playing in the 1998 World Cup?

72. Who called the Polish keeper Jan Tomaszewski a "clown" before the England v Poland 1974 World Cup qualifier?

73. Where did the draw for the 1994 World cup finals take place?

74. Who were the first team to qualify for the 1994 World Cup?

75. What did all the 15 penalties awarded in open play in 1994 have in common?

76. In the 1994 World Cup the referees and linesmen's kit came in which three colours?

77. Up to the 1994 finals, which is the only country to have played in every World Cup tournament?

78. For the first time in the World Cup finals what was awarded for a win in a group match in 1994?

79. The 1994 World Cup mascot "Striker" was a dog created by whom?

80. Who won the Golden Ball award for best player in the 1994 World Cup?

81. Who said:"I don't know how we do it sometimes." When England reached the 1990 World Cup semi-finals?

82. Scotland lost 1-0 to which unfancied team in their first match at the 1990 World Cup?

83. Who is England's top scorer in all World Cup matches?

84. Scotland's manager resigned after the 1986 finals - who was he?

85. Who scored in the Republic of Ireland's shock defeat of Italy in the 1994 World Cup?

86. Who scored the goal in England's shock defeat by the United States in the 1950 World Cup tournament?

87. Who scored the 1,000th World Cup goal in 1978?

88. Which was the first black African country to qualify for the World Cup finals?

89. Why did the English referee Jack Taylor delay the start of the 1974 World Cup final?

90. In the 1970 World Cup what was Bobby Moore accused of stealing in Bogota, Colombia?

76. Silver, gold and pink on a black check background. 77. **Brazil** 78. Three points 79. **Warner Brothers** 80. Romario (Brazil) 81. **Bobby Robson** 82. Costa Rica 83. **Gary Lineker** 84. Alex Ferguson 85. **Ray Houghton** 86. Larry Gaetjens 87. **Robbie Rensenbrink (Holland)** 88. Zaire in 1974 89. He noticed all the midfield and corner flags were missing. 90. A bracelet.

91. Who are currently the only two players to have scored in more than one World Cup Finals?

92. Who is the oldest player to have won a World Cup winners medal?

93. Which African country have qualified for both World Cup Finals that have been held in Mexico?

94. What could Argentina and Uruguay not agree on before the start of the 1930 World Cup final?

95. Spain entered the 1938 World Cup, why did they not compete?

96. In the 1970 World Cup match between England and Brazil who scored Brazil's winning goal?

97. In 1970 England lost to West Germany in the quarter-finals, but who scored the two English goals?

98. Which World Cup tournament was the first to be televised?

99. Who was the first player to score in every game of a World Cup tournament?

100. Which country was eliminated from the 1974 World Cup on goal difference without losing a game?

101. Who was Argentina's chain-smoking manager in the 1978 World Cup?

102. Who is the youngest player ever to have played in the World Cup?

103. Who was Brazil's philosophical captain in the 1982 World Cup?

104. Alf Ramsey was an England player in which World Cup?

105. What was the average age of the England World Cup winning squad in 1966?

91. Pele in 1958 and 1970, Paul Breitner (West Germany) 1974 and 1982.
92. Dino Zoff aged 40 - Italy 93. Morocco 94. They couldn't agree on which ball to
use 95. **Because of the outbreak of the Spanish Civil War.** 96. Jairinho 97.
Martin Peters and Alan Mullery 98. Switzerland 1954 99. Jairinho, Brazil
1970. 100. Scotland 101. **Cesar Luis Menotti** 102. Norman Whiteside -
Northern Ireland 103. **Socrates** 104. 1950 World Cup 105. **Twenty-six and a
half years**

106. Who were the two reserve goalkeepers in England's 1966 squad?

108. How many goals did Jimmy Greaves score in the 1966 World Cup?

109. Who was awarded the Silver Ball trophy for goals and assists in the 1994 World Cup?

110. Who won the Lev Yashin Goalkeeper Award in the 1994 World Cup?

111. What will be the tournament mascot for the French World Cup in 1988?

112. Who countries will co-host the 2002 World Cup?

113. Which European country did Italy beat in the 1934 semi-final?

114. England failed to qualify in 1974 thanks to a 1-1 draw with Poland at Wembley in October 1973. England had already played them in Poland in June of that same year, what was the score?

115. Which countries did Cameroon beat to reach the World Cup quarter-finals in 1990?

116. Prior to the 1994 World Cup which team had appeared in five tournaments but failed to win a game?

117. How many times have Mexico played in the finals?

118. Who topped England's group in the 1986 tournament?

119. What has been Spain's most successful World Cup?

120. Where did they finish?

 Quiz **18** **The World Cup**

121. **Who was the first player banned for drug taking by FIFA in a World Cup?**

122. Who finished top of England's qualifying group in the lead up to the 1990 World Cup?

123. **England drew with the Republic of Ireland in the 1990 World Cup, who scored the goals?**

124. In the 1990 World Cup who replaced David Seaman after he had broken his thumb in training?

125. **Which was the first African country to reach a World Cup quarter-final?**

126. Who presented the Jules Rimet trophy to the Italian captain Combi after his team had won the 1934 World Cup?

127. **In the 1994 qualifiers San Marino lost nine games and drew one. Who was the draw against?**

128. Why did India withdraw from the 1950 World Cup?

129. **Who were the first team to win the World Cup outside of their own continent?**

130. In their opening game of the 1990 World Cup Holland, the favourites, were held to a 1-1 draw, by who?

131. **In the same group the Republic of Ireland also drew 1-1 with Holland, who scored the goals?**

132. Who did Italy beat in the 1934 World Cup Final?

133. **Why were Nigeria disqualified from the 1974 World Cup?**

134. How many players did Brazil use in the 1962 World Cup?

135. **Allan Clarke made his international debut against which team in the 1970 World Cup?**

136. Peter Shilton's World Cup finals debut was against which team in 1982?

137. Ex-England manager Bobby Robson played in which World Cup?

138. In which tournament and against which team did Gordon Banks play his last World Cup game?

139. Who missed a late goalscoring chance for England against Brazil in the 1970 finals?

140. Who managed the 1982 World Cup winning Italian team?

141. How long did it take Bryan Robson to score England's first goal in the 1982 tournament against France?

142. Who finished third in the 1982 World Cup?

143. Having successfully qualified for the 1950 World Cup why did the Scottish team refuse to go?

144. What was the nationality of the linesman who awarded England's third goal in the 1966 World Cup final?

145. North Korea beat which team to progress to the quarter-finals in the 1966 World Cup?

146. Which German defender has scored in two World Cup Finals?

147. Which two Dutch brothers played in the 1978 World Cup Final?

148. In the match for third place in the 1970 World Cup who did West Germany beat 1-0?

149. The first penalty to be awarded in a World Cup final was in which tournament?

150. Which Dutch player had his arm bandaged in the 1978 World Cup final against Argentina?

136. France 137. 1958 138. Brazil 1970 139. Jeff Astle 140. Enzo Bearzot 141. 27 seconds 142. Poland 143. Because they did not win the qualifying group 144. Russian 145. Italy 146. Paul Breitner 147. Willie and Rene Van de Kerkhoff 148. Uruguay 149. 1974 150. Rene Van de Kerkhof

151. Who held Scotland to a 1-1 draw in a first round match during the 1978 World Cup?

152. What was unusual about the two goalkeepers in the 1978 World Cup Final?

153. In the 1982 World Cup which team drew all three of their first round matches?

154. In the 1982 World Cup who beat the hosts 1-0 in the first round?

155. Who scored the goal?

156. Which team were threatened with expulsion from the 1986 World Cup tournament for persistant foul-play?

157. Which two teams were in the third place play-off in the 1986 World Cup - and what was the score?

158. What position did Alf Ramsey play in the 1950 World Cup squad?

159. In England's second game in the 1986 World Cup against Morocco, what injury did Bryan Robson sustain?

160. Who qualified for the 1950 World Cup without having to play a single game?

161. Which city hosted the first World Cup final in 1930?

162. Played 6, lost 6, goals for 1, goals against 22 - the worst record in the World Cup finals. Which team is this?

163. Up to the end of the 1994 finals, Brazil have the best record in the World Cup followed by the Germans. Who are third?

164. Who was the eccentric Colombian goalkeeper in the 1990 World Cup?

165. In which World Cup match did Chelsea's Peter Bonnetti earn his seventh and last England cap?

151. Iran 152. Jan Jongbloed wore number eight shirt and Ubaldo Fillol wore the number seven 153. Italy and Cameroon 154. Northern Ireland 155. Gerry Armstrong 156. Uruguay 157. Belgium anf France. France won 4-2. 158. Right-back 159. Shoulder injury 160. Brazil 161. Montevideo 162. El Salvador 163. Italy 164. Rene Higuita 165. The quarter-final against West Germany-

166. Billy Wright captained England through how many World Cup finals campaigns?

167. **Up to 1994, how many finals matches have New Zealand played?**

168. Who was the youngest player in the England World Cup final team of 1966?

169. **In England's 1970 World Cup quarter-final against West Germany Sir Alf Ramsey made a critical substitution when the German's pulled a goal back, what was it?**

170. In the 1978 World Cup, Scotland beat Holland 3-2 in a first round group match. Who scored for the Scots?

171. **In the same group which two unfancied teams did the Scots lose to and draw with?**

172. Who did the West Germans put six past in a first round group match of the 1978 World Cup?

173. **Who was the first player to be sent off in a World Cup final?**

174. Which England player announced his retirement after the third place play-off in the 1990 World Cup?

175. **Italy, Spain, Holland and Sweden all applied to stage the first World Cup. Why did FIFA ultimately choose Uruguay?**

176. In the 1938 World Cup which country received a bye through to the second round due to Germany's invasion of Austria?

177. **Who was the Russian goalkeeper in the 1958 World Cup?**

178. Why did Gordon Banks miss the 1970 World Cup quarter-final against West Germany?

179. **Patented by the Dutch, 'Total Football' made its debut in which World Cup?**

180. The Soviet Union failed to qualify for the 1974 World Cup after drawing with Chile 0-0 in Moscow and refusing to play the return leg. Why did the Russians refuse to play in Chile?

166. Three 167. **Three** 168. Alan Ball 169. **Bobby Charlton came off for Colin Bell** 170. Archie Gemmill (2, 1 pen) and Kenny Dalglish 171. **Peru and Iran** 172. Mexico 173. **Monzon** 174. Peter Shilton 175. **They were Olympic soccer champions and they promised to underwrite the costs of the competing countries** 176. Sweden 177. **Lev Yashin** 178. Because of food poisoning 179. 1974 180. Because the National Stadium in Chile had been used to house prisoners in Chile's Civil War

181. **Which country knocked Mexico out of the World Cup in the qualifying stages of 1974?**

182. Which Dutchman did the West German Uli Hoeness trip to give Holland a penalty in the 1974 World Cup final?

183. **Where and when was the first World Cup held?**

184. Which three European countries reached the 1986 semi-finals?

185. **Which country became the first to win the World Cup on foreign soil?**

186. Who scored Scotland's only goal in the 1986 finals?

187. **In which World Cup did England make their first appearance?**

188. Which English club ground staged one of the semi-finals in 1966?

189. **Who did England beat in the 1966 semi-final?**

190. Which Arsenal goalkeeper played for Wales in the 1958 World Cup Finals?

191. **Who was sent-off in England's quarter-final against Argentina in 1966?**

192. Geoff Hurst scored a hat-trick in the 1966 Final. Who got England's other goal?

193. **Who scored Brazil's fourth goal in their win over Italy in the 1970 Final?**

194. In which World Cup finals did Zaire made their first appearance?

195. **Who was Scotland's top scorer in the 1974 finals?**

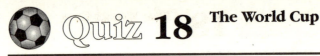
196. What is the highest recorded attendance at a World Cup finals match?

197. **Gary Lineker scored a hat-trick in England's last group game in the 1986 finals. Against which country?**

198. Lineker scored six of England's seven goals in the 1986 finals. Who got the other one?

199. **When Argentina beat England in 1986 which England player was the last to touch the ball before Diego Maradona scored his "hand of God" goal?**

200. Which club did Gary Lineker join after the 1986 finals?

201. **Who scored Argentina's winning goal in the 1986 Final?**

202. Which Chilean goalkeeper feigned injury against Brazil in the qualifying round tie for Italia '90, and was banned from international football for life?

203. **Who scored the only goal for Cameroon in the opening game of the 1990 finals against Argentina?**

204. How many players did Cameroon finish that game with?

205. **Who is the oldest player to score in a World Cup finals match?**

206. Who scored England's winning goal against Egypt to help them through to the second round of the 1990 Finals?

207. **Who scored the Republic of Ireland's winning penalty in the shoot-out against Romania in the 1990 Finals?**

208. Who did Andreas Brehme's shot deflect off to open the scoring for Germany in the 1990 semi-final against England?

209. **The opening game of the 1994 finals was played at Soldier Field. What city is the stadium in?**

210. How many European teams qualified for the quarter-finals in 1994?

Quiz 18

211. Who beat the reigning champions, Germany, in the quarter-finals in 1994?

212. Who scored their goals?

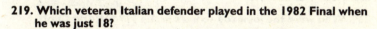

213. Where was the 1994 Final played?

214. Which three Italians missed penalty's in the 1994 Final shoot-out to give Brazil the World Cup?

215. What were England the first to achieve for 32 years in 1966?

216. Who scored West Germany's last-minute equaliser against England in the 1966 Final?

217. Who was the West German goalkeeper in the 1996 Final?

218. Which was the last World Cup Finals that Italy failed to qualify for?

219. Which veteran Italian defender played in the 1982 Final when he was just 18?

220. Who scored Italy's goals in the 1982 Final against West Germany?

221. Who scored the last goal from open play in the 1994 finals?

222. Italy were runners-up in 1994, but where did they finish after the group matches?

223. Holland beat the Republic of Ireland in the second round in 1994. Who got the Dutch's second goal?

224. Italy beat Nigeria 2-1 in the second round of 1994. Who scored both the Italian goals?

225. How many goals did Romario score in the 1994 Finals?

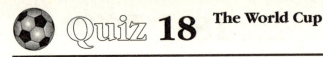
226. Who did Brazil beat in the 1962 World Cup Final?

227. **When did New Zealand make their first appearance in the Finals?**

228. Which two British countries reached the quarter-finals of the World Cup in 1958?

229. **Which country finished third in the 1974 World Cup?**

230. Who pipped England for qualification to the 1978 Finals?

231. **How far did Northern Ireland go in the 1982 Finals?**

232. One of Northern Ireland's stars in 1982 was Gerry Armstrong. Which second division club was he playing for at the time?

233. **When was the last time Wales reached the finals?**

234. What round did they reach?

235. **Who scored the goal that knocked them out?**

236. Up to 1994, have Scotland ever got past the first round of the finals?

237. **What is the record number of goals scored by one player in the finals?**

238. Who holds that record?

239. **Who were the joint top scorers in the 1994 World Cup?**

240. Before playing in 1994 when was Norway's last appearance in the World Cup Finals?

241. Who finished third in the 1990 World Cup Finals?

242. Who beat Bulgaria to finish third in the 1994 World Cup?

243. Who did Argentina beat in a play-off to qualify for the 1994 World Cup Finals?

244. Which two countries qualified ahead of England for the 1994 World Cup Finals?

245. Who missed England's final penalty in the 1990 World Cup semi-final?

246. Who were the first country not to score in a Final?

247. What year was it?

248. Whose goal knocked the U.S.A out of the 1994 World Cup?

249. Which World Cup finals match was the first to be played indoors?

250. Where was that game played?

251. Who succeeded the injured Bryan Robson as England captain in the 1990 World Cup finals?

252. Can you name the other three countries in England's Group One during the 1966 World Cup?

253. All of England's 1966 group games were played at Wembley, except one. Where was that played and who were the two teams?

254. Who is the oldest player to captain a World Cup winning side?

255. Before the start of the 1998 World Cup, who is the last player to score in a Final?

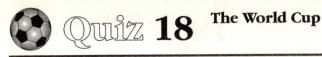

256. Who was the first substitute to score in a World Cup?

257. Which five nations boycotted the first World Cup in 1930 because they were passed over as hosts in favour of Uruguay?

258. Who is the oldest player to score World Cup finals goal?

259. What was unique about the West Germany-Italy final in 1970?

260. Which nation was originally selected as hosts for the 1986 finals and why did they withdraw?

261. Why did Roberto Rojas of Chile incur a life ban after a 1990 qualifying match?

262. Which nation played a World Cup match only two days after the country had been devastated by an earthquake?

263. Who was leading scorer in the 1974 World Cup finals?

264. Who is the only man to play in two World Cup winning sides and to win it again as a manager?

265. Which player scored four goals in one match during the 1986 finals?

266. Which nation qualified for five finals series between 1962 and 1986 yet failed to win any of 16 matches?

267. Why was England's match with Brazil in Sweden in 1958 unique?

268. Who was the first player to score at least five goals in two different World Cups?

269. Who has scored a record number of finals goals?

270. Which nation set a record by schedulling finals matches for 17 different stadia?

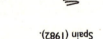

256. Juan Basaguren for Mexico in a 4-0 win over El Salvador on June 7, 1970. 257. Spain, Italy, Sweden, Hungary and Holland 258. Cameroon's Roger Milla. 259. It is the only match in World Cup finals history to produce five extra time goals. 260. Colombia - because of economic difficulties. 261. Goalkeeper Rojas faked injury claiming a flare had hit him causin g the game to be abandoned. 262. Peru - in the 1970 World Cup. 263. Gregorz Lato of Poland with seven goals. 264. Brazil's Mario Zagalo - he played in 1958 and 1962 and was manager in 1970. 265. Emilio Butragueno (Spain) v Denmark in 1986. 266. Bulgaria. 267. It was the first scoreless draw in the finals. 268. Teofilo Cubillas (Peru) in 1970 and 1978. 269. Gerd Muller (West Germany) with 14. 270. Spain (1982).

271. **Which goalkeeper played in a record five World Cups yet appeared on the winning side only once?**

272. Which nation did not qualify for the finals between 1938 and 1974 then reached the next four, finishing third twice?

273. **Who was the first player to score an extra-time goal in a Final?**

274. Which event in World Cup history occurred on March 20, 1966?

275. **Which two pairs of brothers have played in World Cup winning teams?**

276. Who is the only player to represent different nations in a World Cup Final?

277. **Which is the smallest city to host the finals?**

278. Which nation holds the highest goals-per-game average in world cup matches?

279. **Who scored the goal that knocked out Italy in 1966?**

280. Which manager hid in Europe for a month after his team was eliminated from the 1966 World Cup?

281. **Which nation lost 32 successive qualifying matches?**

282. Who refereed the first World Cup Final in 1930?

283. **Who was the first substitute to score three times in a World Cup finals match?**

284. Who finished top scorer in the 1966 finals?

285. **Name the only city to host an entire World Cup finals series.**

286. Which is the only nation to reach the semi-finals four times and have not been beaten?

287. **Why were England uncertain whether their 1986 meeting with Portugal would go ahead?**

288. Who was sent off after a record 55 seconds of a 1986 World Cup match?

289. **Which player scored four goals in a finals match but was still on the losing side?**

290. Which nation won 47 of 48 internationals between 1950 and 1956 yet failed to win the World Cup?

291. **Which was the first Asian country to play in the World Cup?**

292. Which nation's only appearance in the finals resulted in a 6-0 defeat?

293. **Whose ripped shorts fell to his ankles seconds after he scored from a penalty in a 1938 semi-final?**

294. Which two teams were involved in a 7-3 match in the group stages of the 1958 tournament?

295. **Who was the first player to score in an Olympic Final and a World Cup Final ?**

296. Who were the first country to win the World Cup in a penalty shoot-out?

297. **What year was it?**

298. Who missed a penalty in his 100th appearance for his country in the 1978 World Cup Finals?

299. **Who was England's goalkeeper when they drew 0-0 with Brazil in the 1958 Finals?**

300. Who beat the hosts Argentina in the group stages of the 1978 World Cup Finals?

286. Argentina. 287. **The Portuguese players had been on strike in a row over bonuses.** 288. Jose Batista(Uruguay) v Scotland. 289. **Ernst Willimowski (Poland) against France in 1938.** 290. Hungary. 291. **The Dutch East Indies(now Indonesia) who qualified for the 1938 finals.** 292. The Dutch East Indies, crushed by Hungary in 1938. 293. **Italy's Giuseppe Meazza.** 294. France and Paraguay. 295. **Pedro Cea of Uruguay in 1924 and 1930.** 296. Brazil 297. 1994 298. Kazimierz Deyna 299. **Colin McDonald** 300. Italy

301. Who finished ahead of Brazil in the group stages of the 1978 World Cup finals?

302. Which Argentinian scored in the 1990 World Cup semi-final?

303. Who were in West Germany's group in the 1978 World Cup?

304. Who beat Mexico and drew with West Germany in the 1978 finals?

305. Who finished third in the 1978 World Cup?

306. Who conceded 12 goals in their three group matches in the 1978 World Cup?

307. Who scored Argentina's three goals in the 1978 Final?

308. Who scored Holland's consolation goal in the 1978 Final?

319. Which goalkeeper saved two penalties in the 1974 World Cup finals?

310. Who scored for Scotland in three World Cup finals?

311. Who beat West Germany in the group stages of the 1974 World Cup?

312. Who played in three World Cup's for Brazil, scoring nine goals?

313. Who is the only player to score in every game of a World Cup finals series when he scored seven in the 1970 Finals?

314. Paulo Rossi scored a hat-trick when Italy beat Brazil 3-2 in the second stage of the 1982 Finals. Who scored Brazil's two goals?

315. Who did Scotland beat 5-2 in the 1982 World Cup finals?

301. Austria 302. Claudio Caniggia **303. Poland, Tunisia, Mexico 304.** Tunisia
305. Brazil 306. Mexico **307. Mario Kempes (2), Bertoni 308.** Dirk Nanninga
309. Jan Tomaszewski 310. Joe Jordan (1974,1978,1982) **311. East Germany**
312. Jairzinho **313. Jairzinho** 314. Socrates and Falcao **315. New Zealand**

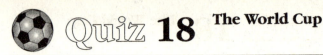 Quiz **18** The World Cup

316. Who scored Scotland's goal in their 4-1 defeat to of Brazil in 1982?

317. Which two England strikers both scored two goals in the 1982 finals?

318. Against who did England draw their two games with in the second stage of the 1982 World Cup?

319. Which players came on as substitutes for England in their second stage match against Spain?

320. Who scored West Germany's consolation goal in the 1982 Final?

321. Northern Ireland reached the second stage of the 1982 finals. Who were in Northern Ireland's group in that second stage?

322. Who did Italy beat in the semi-final to reach the 1982 World Cup Final?

323. Who missed the final stages of the 1962 World Cup through injury?

324. Which Frenchman gave his name to the first World Cup trophy?

325. Who captained West Germany to the 1990 World Cup?

326. How much - in Francs - did the original World Cup trophy cost?

327. How many people attended the first World Cup?

328. In the 1934 World Cup Finals, 12 of the competing nations were from Europe. Who were the other four teams present?

329. Who scored England's goal in the third place play-off in 1990?

330. Which two players scored hat-tricks in the 1990 World Cup?

316. David Narey 317. **Paul Mariner and Trevor Francis** 318. West Germany and Spain 319. **Kevin Keegan and Trevor Brooking** 320. Paul Breitner 321. France and Austria 322. Poland 323. **Pelé** 324. Jules Rimet 325. **Lothar Matthaus** 326. 50,000 Francs 327. **343,500** 328. Egypt, Argentina, Brazil and USA 329. **David Platt** 330. Thomas Skuhravy and Michel

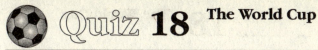

331. Who did Sweden beat 8-0 in the second round of the 1938 Finals - this country's last appearance in the tournament's finals?

332. Who scored Italy's only goal in the 1990 quarter-final against the Republic of Ireland?

333. Who was the England manager in the 1950 Finals?

334. Who did England beat in the second round of the 1986 World Cup Finals?

335. Who were clear favourites to win the 1954 World Cup?

336. What was that team's nickname?

337. Which Brazilian made his first finals appearance in 1958?

338. Who was Northern Ireland's goalkepper inthe 1958 Finals?

339. Who hosted the 1954 World Cup?

340. Who beat South Korea 9-0 in the group stage of the 1954 World Cup?

341. Which countries scored 17 goals in two group matches in the 1954 World Cup?

342. Which two countries played each other twice in the 1954 tournament?

343. Which two nations contested a 7-5 quarter-final in the 1954 Finals?

344. Who beat West Germany 6-3 to finish third in the 1958 World Cup?

345. Which player scored four goals against Denmark in the 1986 finals?

346. Who beat Wales in the quarter-finals of the 1958 Finals?

347. Who was the English referee in the 1974 World Cup Final?

348. What was so unusual about the 1974 World Cup Final?

349. How many British Isles countries reached the 1958 finals?

350. Who was sent-off against Brazil in the 1982 tournament?

351. Who did England lose to in the 1962 quarter-finals?

352. Which two South American countries reached the 1962 quarter-finals?

353. Who replaced Gary Lineker in England's 3-0 defeat of Poland in the 1986 Finals?

354. Who scored Portugal's goal in their 1-0 win over England in 1986?

355. Which Englishmen led Sweden to the 1958 World Cup Final?

356. Who became the first country to win the World Cup four times?

357. Which two teams were involved in the 'Battle of Santiago' in the 1962 World Cup?

358. Who hosted the 1962 World Cup?

359. How many teams competed in the 1950 World Cup Finals?

360. Who did Italy beat in the 1938 World Cup Final?

361. What was the score in the 1938 Final?

362. Who hosted the 1954 World Cup?

363. Who hosted the 1958 World Cup?

364. The England team were without three important players in the 1958 World Cup Finals, Why?

365. Brazil played Wales in the 1958 Finals, what was the score?

366. What was the average goals per game in the first World Cup tournament in 1930?

367. In what year did FIFA first moot the idea of staging a World Cup?

368. Which three countries made a bid to stage the subsequently aborted 1942 World Cup?

369. In the 1934 World Cup qualifying match between Hungary and Bulgaria, who was the referee?

370. Before travelling to the 1950 World Cup in Brazil where did the England team train?

371. When Northern Ireland qualified for the 1958 finals what did the Irish FA order the team not to do?

372. Which country did FIFA allow back into the World Cup tournament in 1954?

373. Who was Northern Ireland's manager in the 1958 World Cup finals?

374. What was the score in the 1958 World Cup final?

375. Who was the assistant manager of the 1994 Republic of Ireland World Cup squad?

1. **Who was the first professional player to move from an English club to Italy?**

2. Which were the first Italian club to buy a player from England?

3. **Who was the first player to transfer from Scotland to Italy, with a move from Hibernian to Juventus?**

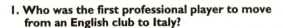

4. Who moved from English football to AC Milan in June 1961?

5. **Who moved from English football to Torino in 1961?**

6. Who moved from Aston Villa to Italy in 1961 for £85,000?

7. **Who was the first person to move from England to Germany?**

8. Who moved from WBA to Real Madrid in 1979?

9. **Which player moved from Manchester City to Werder Bremen in 1979?**

10. How much did Liam Brady cost Juventus when he left Arsenal in 1980?

11. **Trevor Francis moved to which foreign club for £900,000?**

12. Who was the first £1m player to move abroad from a British club?

13. **Which two players moved from English clubs to AEK Athens in 1983?**

14. Which club did Mark Hateley move from when he joined AC Milan?

15. **How much did Ray Wilkins cost AC Milan when he joined them in 1984?**

1. **Eddie Firmani** 2. Sampdoria 3. **Joe Baker** 4. Jimmy Greaves 5. **Denis Law** 6. Gerry Hitchens 7. **Kevin Keegan** 8. Laurie Cunningham 9. **Dave Watson** 10. Juventus 11. **Sampdoria** 12. Luther Blissett to AC Milan 13. **Trevor Ross and Tommy Langley** 14. Portsmouth 15. **£150,000**

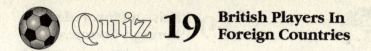
16. Which two players moved from Aston Villa to Bari in 1985?

17. **How much did Ian Rush cost Juventus when he left Liverpool in 1987?**

18. Which Italian club did Paul Elliott join in 1987?

19. **How much did David Platt cost when he moved to Bari?**

20. How much did Paul Gascoigne cost Lazio when he moved to Italy?

21. **How much did Des Walker cost Sampdoria when he joined them in 1992?**

22. Who played for AC Milan and Verona from 1981?

23. **Which Italian club did amateur centre forward Norman Adcock join in 1945 to become the first ever player to move to play in Europe?**

24. Which British export became the French First Division's top scorer in the 1994 season?

25. **Which former Arsenal championship winner moved to Stabaeck in Norway?**

26. Which two Brits teamed up for the same club in Italy for the 1996-97 season?

27. **Which player joined Reggiana in the 1996-97 season from an English club?**

28. Ted McMinn moved from Rangers to which Spanish side in 1987?

29. **Mick Robinson moved from QPR to which Spanish side in 1987?**

30. Which two British internationals moved abroad in May 1986?

Quiz 19 — British Players In Foreign Countries

31. **Who moved from Celtic to Nantes in 1987?**

32. Which ex-Manchester United player moved to Kaizer Chiefs in South Africa in January 1988?

33. **How much did Steve Archibald cost Barcelona when he moved from Tottenham?**

34. Which club did Mark McGhee move to from Aberdeen?

35. **Which club did Andy King join from Everton in 1984?**

36. Which club did Raphael Meade join when he left Arsenal?

37. **Which foreign club did John Richards join in 1983?**

38. Who did Peter Barnes join in 1982 when he moved from Leeds?

39. **Who moved from Liverpool to Lucerne in a free transfer in 1983?**

40. Watford's Gerry Armstrong moved to which foreign club in 1983?

41. **How much was the transfer fee when Graeme Souness moved to Sampdoria?**

42. Eric Black joined which French side when he moved from Aberdeen for £200,000 in 1986?

43. **Dale Tempest joined Lokeren from which English club?**

44. Gary Owen moved to which foreign club from WBA in 1986?

45. **Louie Donowa moved from Norwich to which Spanish club in 1986?**

31. **Mo Johnston** 32. Gary Bailey 33. **£1,000,000** 34. SV Hamburg 35. **Cabuur** 36. Sporting Lisbon 37. **Maritimo Funchal** 38. Real Betis 39. **David Fairclough** 40. Real Mallorca 41. **£650,000** 42. Metz 43. **Huddersfield** 44. Panionios 45. **La Coruna**

46. Tony Woodcock left Arsenal for which German club in 1986?

47. **Sammy McIlroy left Manchester City for which foreign club in 1986?**

48. Tottenham gave Ally Dick a free transfer to which Dutch team in 1986?

49. **Joe Jakub joined which Dutch team for £20,000 in 1986?**

50. Garry Brooke moved to which club when he left Norwich in 1987?

51. **Murdo McLeod joined which German side in 1987?**

52. Which club did Frank Stapleton join on a free transfer to in 1987?

53. **George O'Boyle moved from Linfield to which French club in 1987?**

54. Which foreign club did Tony Sealey join when he left Leicester in 1987?

55. **Dave Swindlehurst joined Anorthosis from which club in 1987?**

56. Ex-Norwich player John Devine moved to which club in September 1987?

57. **Gary Waddock joined which French club in January 1988 after he left QPR?**

58. Which French team signed Ian Wallace when he left Nottingham Forest in 1984?

59. **Bob Latchforrd left Swansea on a free transfer to join which club?**

60. Which team signed Jim Bett when he left Glasgow Rangers in 1983?

Quiz 19 — British Players In Foreign Countries

61. **Who moved from the Premiership to Malaysia in 1996?**

62. Tony Marchi left Tottenham for which foreign side in 1961?

63. **John Charles joined which Italian side for #70,000 in 1962?**

64. Mick Walsh left QPR for which European team in 1980?

65. **How much did Trevor Francis cost Sampdoria when he joined them in 1982?**

66. Francois Van Der Elst left West Ham for which side in 1983?

67. **Which two Tottenham players from the 1980s moved to France?**

68. What are the four Italian teams that Liam Brady played for?

69. **Which clubs did David Platt play for in Italy?**

70. How many seasons did Denis Law spend in Italy?

71. **How many seasons did Trevor Francis spend at Sampdoria?**

72. How many games did Jimmy Greaves play in Italy?

73. **Who scored 87 goals in six seasons in Italy from 1957-63?**

74. Frank Ratcliffe moved from Aldershot to which serie B side for the 1949-50 season, where he scored 18 goals in 27 games?

75. **In which season did Ian Rush play in Italy?**

61. Tony Cottee **62.** Lanerossi Vicenza **63.** AS Roma **64.** Porto **65.** £900,000 **66.** Lokeren **67.** Glenn Hoddle and Chris Waddle **68.** Juventus, Sampdoria, Inter Milan, Ascoli **69.** Bari, Juventus, Sampdoria **70.** 1 (1961-62) **71.** 4 **72.** 10 (with 9 goals) **73.** John Charles **74.** Alessandria **75.** 1987-88

76. What was the name of the team that Gary Lineker played for in Japan?

77. Which country did Richard Gough leave Rangers to play in after the 1996-97 season?

78. Which former Watford striker had a spell at French club Nantes?

79. Which American team did Rodney Marsh play for?

80. Which team did Charlton's Mike Flanagan play for in America?

81. Which former Welsh international had a spell at Vancouver Whitecaps?

82. With which Turkish team did Les Ferdinand have a loan spell with?

83. Dean Saunders spent a season at which foreign club before moving back to Nottingham Forest?

84. Dalian Atkinson moved to which foreign club when he left Aston Villa?

85. Which Scot played for Borussia Dortmund in the 1996-97 season?

86. Mo Johnston spent the 1996-97 season playing where?

87. Chris Woods was playing in which country before playing for Southampton in the 1996-97 season?

88. How many goals did David Platt score in his first season in Italy?

89. Who moved to Paris St Germain after three years at AC Milan?

90. Josiah (Paddy) Sloan moved from Sheffield United to which foreign team for the 1948-49 season?

76. Nagoya Grampus Eight **77. America** 78. Mo Johnston **79. Tampa Bay Rowdies** 80. New England Tea Men **81. Terry Yorath** 82. Beşiktaş 83. **Galatasaray** 84. Fenerbache **85. Paul Lambert** 86. America **87. America** 88. 11, in 29 games 89. **Ray Wilkins** 90. AC Milan

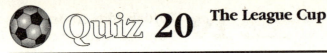

1. **In which year did the first final of the League Cup take place?**

2. In which year did the first Wembley final take place?

3. **Who were the winners of the first League Cup?**

4. Who were the Second Division underdogs who reached the 1961 final, and led 2-0 after the first leg?

5. **Who scored the winning goal in the first-ever League Cup final?**

6. Who was the Spurs manager who refused to let his side take part in the first League Cup?

7. **Which Fourth Division side reached the 1962 final?**

8. Who put the holders out of the competition in 1962?

9. **The 1961 final was completed in which month?**

10. Which Villa player was the top scorer in the 1961 competition?

11. **Who were the first winners of the League Cup who did not play their football in the top flight?**

12. Who holds the all-time scoring record in the League Cup?

13. **Which Welsh international scored a brace for Birmingham in the 1963 final?**

14. Which club reached the final in 1964 and 1965?

15. **Which club, now no longer in the League, reached the fifth round in 1964 only to be beaten 6-0 by West Ham?**

1. 1961 2. 1967 3. **Aston Villa** 4. Rotherham 5. **Peter McParland** 6. Bill Nicholson 7. **Rochdale** 8. Ipswich 9. **September** 10. Gerry Hitchens 11. **Norwich in 1962** 12. Geoff Hurst 13. **Ken Leek** 14. Leicester City 15. **Workington**

16. Which future England manager scored a penalty in the 1965 final?

17. **Who was the legendary English goalkeeper who played in both the 1964 and 1965 finals?**

18. Which club reached the final three times in five years between 1966 and 1970?

19. **Which Stoke player scored ten goals in the 1963-64 season?**

20. Which Premiership striker's father was the top scorer in the 1964-65 season while playing for Aston Villa?

21. **Whose brainchild was the League Cup, leading it to be labelled his 'folly'?**

22. In which year was the introduction of a European place for the winners?

23. **Which two clubs were the only teams not to enter the 1967 competition?**

24. Which club won the 1967 competition, but could not qualify for Europe because they were not a First Division club?

25. **Which Leeds full-back scored the only goal of a dour 1968 final?**

26. Which team lost in the final in 1968 and 1969?

27. **Which television commentator played in goals for Arsenal in the 1969 final?**

28. Which Swindon player scored a brace in the 1969 final to shock Arsenal?

29. **Who were the first club to win a place in Europe through the competition?**

30. Which Manchester City stalwart scored a penalty in the 1970 semi-final derby clash?

16. Terry Venables 17. **Gordon Banks** 18. WBA 19. **John Ritchie** 20. Mark Hateley 21. **Alan Hardaker** 22. 1967 23. Liverpool and Everton 24. QPR 25. **Terry Cooper** 26. Arsenal 27. **Bob Wilson** 28. Don Rogers 29. **Arsenal** 30. Francis Lee

31. Which WBA striker scored their only goal in the 1970 final?

32. In which year did Tottenham reach their first final?

33. In which year did the Football League reject a £600,000 offer for sponsorship of the competition?

34. Which Tottenham player was the top scorer in the 1970-71 and 1971-72 campaigns?

35. Which Stoke keeper saved a penalty in the 1972 semi-final to give them their first visit to Wembley?

36. How many games did West Ham and Stoke play in the 1972 semi-finals before a winner was finally decided?

37. Who was the Stoke manager who led his team to glory in 1972?

38. Which Stoke player, at the age of 35, scored his first goal in 18 months when he hit the winner in the 1972 finals?

39. Who were the first club to win the trophy twice?

40. Which England international scored Tottenham's only goal in the 1973 final?

41. Who was the Wolverhampton hero when he replaced Phil Parkes in goal and pulled off a series of stunning saves to win the 1974 final?

42. Which Manchester City player caused controversy when he left the field immediately after losing the 1974 final, without collecting his loser's medal?

43. Which future Watford manager scored the opener for Wolves in the 1974 final?

44. In which year were there no First Division sides in the semi-finals?

45. Which Fourth Division side reached the semi-finals in 1975 after beating Leeds and Newcastle United?

31. **Jeff Astle** 32. 1971 33. 1971 34. Martin Chivers 35. **Gordon Banks** 36. Four 37. **Tony Waddington** 38. George Eastham 39. **Tottenham Hotspur** 40. Ralph Coates 41. **Gary Pierce** 42. Rodney Marsh 43. **Kenny Hibbitt** 44. 1975 45. **Chester City**

46. Who was the Villa manager who led them to victory in 1975 after two previous final defeats?

47. **Which two England internationals scored Manchester City's goals in the 1976 final victory over Newcastle?**

48. Which Villa player and future manager was the top scorer in the 1976-77 campaign?

49. **Which Welsh international scored a last-minute goal to give Villa a second replay in the 1977 final against Everton?**

50. For how many minutes did Aston Villa and Everton play to decide the 1977 competition?

51. **Which 18-year-old keeper was drafted in to keep goal for Forest against Liverpool in the 1978 final?**

52. Who did Phil Thompson bring down in a profesional foul to give Forest and penalty and eventually victory in the 1978 final?

53. **Which team upset Liverpool in the 1979 championship when they beat the favourites in the second round?**

54. Which bargain basement striker, bought from a local non-League club, scored a brace for Forest in the final against Southampton in 1979?

55. **Which club reached three consecutive finals at the end of the Seventies?**

56. Which fellow First Division side did Arsenal beat 7-0 in the second round of the 1979-80 competition?

57. **Who was the Liverpool keeper who brought down Garry Birtles in the semi-final of the 1979-80 competition?**

58. Which former winners reached the semi-finals in 1980 while still a Third Divison side?

59. **Which Wolves player took advantage of confusion between Peter Shilton and David Needham to score the only goal of the 1980 final?**

60. Who won their first League Cup in 1981?

61. Who scored West Ham's only goal in the replay for the 1981 final?

62. Which Liverpool player was the top scorer for the 1980-81 competition?

63. How many consecutive League Cups did Liverpool claim?

64. By what name was the League Cup known between 1982 and 1986?

65. Which Liverpool player scored a brace in the 1982 final, when the Reds beat Tottenham in extra-time?

66. Which former Liverpool keeper was beaten three times by his old club in the 1982 final?

67. Which Liverpool manager led them to victory in 1983 and then retired?

68. When Burnley beat Bury 8-4 in the 1982-83 competition, how many different players scored for Burnley?

69. Who was the Burnley manager sacked by his club on the day of their fifth round victory over Tottenham Hotspur?

70. What was the Wembley crowd when Liverpool met Manchester United in the 1983 final?

71. Which Manchester United player was the competition's top scorer in 1982-83?

72. Who scored the opening goal in the 1983 final, giving Manchester United an early lead?

73. At which ground was the 1984 replay held?

74. Which Third Division side held Liverpool to a draw at Anfield in the 1984 semi-finals?

75. In which year did Liverpool meet Everton at Wembley for the first time in history?

61. Paul Goddard 62. Kenny Dalglish **63. Four** 64. Milk Cup **65. Ronnie Whelan** 66. Ray Clemence **67. Bob Paisley** 68. Eight - one of which was a Bury player. **69. Brian Miller** 70. 100,000 **71. Steve Coppell** 72. Norman Whiteside **73. Maine Road** 74. Walsall **75. 1984**

76. Which two teams met in a 'derby' game in the 1985 semi-finals?

77. **Which team won the 1985 competition in the same year that they were relegated from the First Division?**

78. Whose own goal gave Norwich victory in 1985?

79. **Who ended Liverpool's amazing run in the competition when they beat them 1-0 in the third round of the 1984-85 competition?**

80. Who played in goal for Norwich in their victory over Sunderland in the 1985 final, winning his second winner's medal?

81. **Who won their first major trophy when they triumphed in the 1986 final?**

82. Which First Division team did Fourth Division Swindon beat in the third round of the 1985-86 competition?

83. **Whose goal for QPR at Loftus Road eventually gave them a place in the 1986 final?**

84. What was the final score when Oxford beat QPR in the 1986 final?

85. **Who began their sponsorship of the League Cup in 1987?**

86. Which First Division team was beaten by Fourth Division Cambridge in the second round of the 1986-87 tournament?

87. **Who were Chelsea beaten by in the third round of the 1986-87 tournament?**

88. Who scored all three goals for Tottenham when they met Arsenal in the 1987 semi-finals?

89. **Who scored a brace for Arsenal in the 1987 final, giving them the cup on their third Wembley visit?**

90. After which final was the League Cup trophy broken?

91. **Which club lifted their ban on away fans in order to compete in the 1987-88 competition, and went on to win the tournament?**

92. Who were Luton playing in the 1987-88 quarter-finals when crowd trouble broke out?

93. **Who was the replacement keeper who saved a penalty for Luton in the 1988 final?**

94. Who scored a brace for Luton as they won the 1988 cup against Arsenal?

95. **Who took the penalty for Arsenal in the 1988 final that would have given them a two-goal lead?**

96. Which Forest player finished the 1988-89 competition as top scorer?

97. **Which Fourth Division side put First Division Middlesbrough out of the 1988-89 competition?**

98. Which Third Division side reached the 1989 semi-finals only to be beaten by Nottingham Forest in extra-time?

99. **Whose extra-time goal gave Nottingham Forest a place in the 1989 final?**

100. Who did Luton beat in the semi-finals of the 1988-89 competition?

101. **Who scored the goals for Forest in their 3-1 victory over Luton in the 1989 final?**

102. Which scorer in the 1989 final later became a member of the Crazy Gang?

103. **Nottingham Forest's fifth visit to the League Cup final came in which year?**

104. Which Fourth Division side drew 1-1 at Stamford Bridge before winning the second leg in 1989-90?

105. **Who put six goals past West Ham in their semi-final first leg in 1990?**

106. Who scored the only goal of the 1990 final?

107. Who sponsored the League Cup in 1991 and 1992?

108. Who hit a hat-trick for Manchester United when they beat Arsenal in the fourth round of the 1990-91 competition?

109. Which Coventry hat-trick man from the 1990-91 quarter-finals later played for Blackburn?

110. Whose hat-trick for Manchester United in the 1990-91 quarter-finals put out Southampton?

111. Who did Sheffield Wednesday beat in the semi-finals of the 1990-91 tournament?

112. Who scored the only goal of the 1991 final?

113. What was the aggregate score when Sheffield Wednesday beat Chelsea in the 1991 semi-finals?

114. How many of Manchester United's League Cup final team of 1991 were still at the club in 1997?

115. Peterborough United put out which two top-flight teams in the 1991-92 competition?

116. Which Tranmere player was top scorer in the 1991-92 competition?

117. Who scored his 100th goal for Manchester United in the 1992 final?

118. Which Second Division team reached the 1992 semi-finals, only to lose to Manchester United in extra-time?

119. Which teams contested the 1993 FA and League Cup finals?

120. Scarborough beat which Premiership team 3-0 in the second leg of the second round of the 1992-93 tournament?

121. **Who were the only non-Premiership side in the 1992-93 quarter-finals?**

122. Who scored Arsenal's only goal when they scraped through against Scarborough in the fourth round of the 1992-93 competition?

123. **Who scored a brace for Sheffield Wednesday when they beat Blackburn in the 1992-93 semi-finals?**

124. Who scored Wednesday's goal in the 1993 final, which they eventually lost 2-1?

125. **Who scored Arsenal's equaliser when they beat Sheffield Wednesday in the 1993 final?**

126. Who scored the winner for Arsenal in the 1993 final, but then had his arm broken when Tony Adams dropped him while celebrating?

127. **Who began their sponsorship of the League Cup in the 1992-93 season?**

128. Aston Villa won the trophy in 1994. How many times had they won it before?

129. **Who scored all five goals when Liverpool beat Fulham in the second round (second leg) in 1993-94?**

130. Who scored the Manchester United winner against Portsmouth to give them a semi-final place?

131. **Who were the only non-Premiership side to reach the 1994 semi-finals?**

132. Who did Manchester United beat in the semi-finals of the 1993-94 competition?

133. **What score was the 1994 semi-final first leg between Tranmere and Aston Villa?**

134. Who scored the Villa goal against Tranmere in the second leg of the 1994 semi-final, which took the game to penalties?

135. **Who was the Villa goalkeeper who saved a penalty against Tranmere to give them a 1994 final berth?**

121. **Cambridge Utd** 122. Nigel Winterburn 123. **Paul Warhurst** 124. John Harkes 125. **Paul Merson** 126. Steve Morrow 127. **Coca-Cola** 128. Three 129. **Robbie Fowler** 130. Brian McClair 131. **Tranmere** 132. Sheffield Wed 133. 3-1 134. Dalian Atkinson 135. **Mark Bosnich**

136. Who scored two goals for Villa in the 1994 final against Manchester United?

137. Which player was shown the red card in the 1994 final?

138. Who put Leeds out of the competition at the second round stage in 1994/95?

139. Which two players scored twice when Crystal Palace beat Aston Villa in the fourth round of the 1994/95 competition?

140. Who scored the Bolton goal which gave them their first semi-final place, in the 1995 tournament?

141. Who was the leading scorer in the 1994-95 tournament?

142. Who scored the goal which gave Bolton victory over Swindon in 1994-95, booking their place in the final?

143. Who scored Liverpool's two goals as they progressed from the 1994-95 semi-finals?

144. Who did Liverpool beat in the 1994-95 semi-finals?

145. Which Liverpool star played against the Reds in the 1995 final?

146. Who scored the goals for Liverpool in the 1995 final?

147. Whose screamer gave Bolton some consolation in the 1995 final?

148. What was the final score in the 1995 final between Liverpool and Bolton?

149. How many appearances have Aston Villa made in the final?

150. Who were Villa's opponents in the 1996 final?

136. Dean Saunders. 137. Andrei Kanchelskis. 138. Mansfield 139. Chris Armstrong and Gareth Southgate 140. David Lee. 141. Jan - Aage Fjortoft 142. John McGinlay 143. Robbie Fowler 144. Crystal Palace 145. Jason McAteer 146. Steve McManaman 147. Alan Thompson 148. 2-1 149. Seven 150. Leeds

151. What was the final aggregate score when Charlton beat Wimbledon in the second round of the 1995-96 competition?

152. Which minnows put Manchester United out of the 1995-96 Cup?

153. Which Yorkshire side put Nottingham Forest out of the 1995-96 tournament?

154. A goal from which veteran gave Reading victory over Southampton in the fourth round in 1995-96?

155. Who was sent off in the 1995-96 quarter-final between Arsenal and Newcastle?

156. Who scored a brace in the 1995-96 quarter-final between Arsenal and Newcastle?

157. Who scored the only goal in the Midlands derby quarter-final between Villa and Wolves in 1995-96?

158. What was the aggregate score in the 1995-96 semi-final between Birmingham and Leeds?

159. Which two Africans were on the score-sheet when Leeds beat Birmingham in the 1995-96 semi-finals?

160. Who scored a brace for Arsenal in their semi-final clash with Aston Villa in 1995-96?

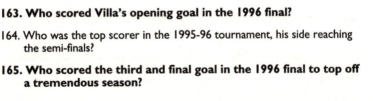

161. Who netted two for Aston Villa when they met Arsenal in the 1995-96 semi-finals?

162. Who played in goal for Leeds in the 1996 final when they lost 3-0 to Aston Villa?

163. Who scored Villa's opening goal in the 1996 final?

164. Who was the top scorer in the 1995-96 tournament, his side reaching the semi-finals?

165. Who scored the third and final goal in the 1996 final to top off a tremendous season?

151. 8-7 152. York City **153. Bradford City** 154. Trevor Morley **155. David Ginola** 156. Ian Wright **157. Tommy Johnson** 158. 5-1 **159. Tony Yeboah and Phil Masinga** 160. Dennis Bergkamp **161. Dwight Yorke** 162. John Lukic **163. Savo Milosevic** 164. Ian Wright **165. Dwight Yorke**

166. Which Second Division side reached the semi-finals of the 1996-97 tournament?

167. Which player, who had been at both clubs, was sent off in the 1996-97 clash between Birmingham and Coventry?

168. How many goals did Middlesbrough put past Hereford in the second round in 1996-97?

169. Which Premiership side did York City put out of the 1996-97 tournament?

170. Which side gave Chelsea a scare in 1996-97 when they won 3-1 at Stamford Bridge?

171. Who did Charlton hold to a draw at the Valley in the 1996-97 season?

172. Who put holders Villa out of the 1996-97 tournament?

173. Who did Middlesbrough beat in the quarter-finals of the 1996-97 competition?

174. Who scored Leicester's only goal when they overcame Ipswich in the 1996-97 quarter-finals?

175. Who scored the winner when Stockport beat Southampton to reach the 1996-97 semi-finals?

176. What was the aggregate score when Middlesbrough beat Stockport in the 1996-97 semi-finals?

177. Whose goal gave Leicester a win over Wimbledon in the semi-finals in 1996-97 on the away goals rule?

178. Who was the Stockport manager who led them into the Coca-Cola Cup semi-finals?

179. Who scored the opening goal of the Wimbledon v Leicester semi-final in 1997?

180. In what month was the final of the 1996-97 competition held?

1. **Which club plays at the Underhill Stadium?**

2. Which club's stadium has terraces called Pontefract Road End and Spion Kop?

3. **To which club's ground is Bordesley the nearest railway station?**

4. Which club plays their home games at Dean Court?

5. **Which club plays at Twerton Park?**

6. Which club's ground has a 22, 085 capacity and has a terrace called Bee Hole Lane End?

7. **What is the name of Bury's stadium?**

8. Which team plays at Ninian Park?

9. **Which country play their international football and rugby union games at the same stadium?**

10. Who play their home games at Brunton Park?

11. **Which ground had temporary seating in the Shed End in 1995-96?**

12. Whose club's ground was the first to go all-seater in England?

13. **Who play their home games at Belle Vue?**

14. Which club's ground is the nearest to Anfield?

15. **There are two grounds in England which each share their names with two clubs. Who are the teams?**

1. **Barnet** 2. Barnsley 3. **St. Andrew's (Birmingham)** 4. Bournemouth 5. **Bristol Rovers** 6. Burnley (Turf Moor) 7. **Gigg Lane** 8. Cardiff 9. **Wales** 10. Carlisle 11. **Stamford Bridge** 12. Coventry 13. **Doncaster** 14. Goodison Park 15. **Newcastle and Exeter (St. James's Park); Hartlepool and Stoke (Victoria Ground)**

16. Which team were facing a possible ground share with Chelsea, but managed to save their ground?

17. **At which ground can you buy a fanzine called Brian Moore's Head (Looks Uncanily Like The London Planetarium)?**

18. Which team's ground is situated in Cleethorpes?

19. **Name Hartlepool United's stadium.**

20. Name Leyton Orient's ground.

21. **Which club play their home games at Sincil Bank?**

22. Which ground in 1994 had only 0.0711% of the capacity (32 seats) for the disabled?

23. **Which club plays at Glanford Park?**

24. Name Oldham Athletic's ground.

25. **Which team play their home games at London Road?**

26. Which team plays their home games at the Millmoor Ground?

27. **Which team has a stand for away fans called the Stone's Best Bitter Stand?**

28. Which team's stadium is on the banks of the river Severn?

29. **Which Premiership ground has a Clock End?**

30. Who play their home games at Plainmoor?

31. **Which club play at Prenton Park, which has a stand called the Cowshed?**

32. Which Premiership club's stadium is named the Boleyn Ground?

33. **Which ground holds the record for the highest crowd for a friendly?**

34. Which team's record attendance of 23,002 against QPR in 1949 came when they were a non-league side?

35. **Which ground has stands named after John Ireland, Jack Harris and Stan Cullis?**

36. Whose home stadium is the Racehorse Ground?

37. **What is Wycombe Wanderers's ground called?**

38. Which team play their home games at Bootham Cresent?

39. **In which year did Wembley first stage the FA Cup final?**

40. Which team's former ground were called Oozebooth, Pleasington Cricket Ground and Alexandra Meadow?

41. **At what ground were the first floodlights introduced in October 1878?**

42. At what ground was the first match to have a gate higher than 10,000 for a match outside Glasgow?

43. **Which club ground's nearest railway station is Castle station?**

44. Where was the first English FA Cup final held?

45. **Where was the only official FA Cup final during the First World War held?**

46. Which club moved ground in 1997-98 after 102 years at Burnden Park?

47. **When did Wembley Stadium first introduce floodlights?**

48. Whose 1997-98 Premiership ground is called the Reebok Stadium?

49. **Since which year has every Scottish FA Cup final been played at Hampden?**

50. In what year did Wembley get the monopoly for all England home internationals?

51. **Which ground held the first ever home England international in 1873?**

52. Where was the first Welsh home international held, in 1877?

53. **Where were the two semi-finals played in the 1966 World Cup?**

54. What were the four quarter-final grounds in the 1966 World Cup?

55. **Where did England play their third place play-off in the 1990 World Cup?**

56. Which club played their final game at the Manor Ground in 1996-97?

57. **What was the ground, other than Wembley, that was used for Group A in Euro 96?**

58. At what ground was the second semi-final in Euro 96 played?

59. **At what ground did Denmark play all of their Euro 96 group matches?**

60. Which were the four grounds in Euro 96 that were not used for the quarter-finals?

61. Which British club play their home games at Gayfield Park?

62. Zampa Road is the address of which English ground?

63. At what ground was the first Match of the Day televised from?

64. At which ground were Manchester United when they lost out to Blackburn on the final day of the 1994-95 season?

65. At which ground is the National Football Museum?

66. At which ground did Huddersfield gain promotion to the First Division in 1995?

67. Before Old Trafford in May 1997, where was the last ground other than Wembley, to hold an England international?

68. Which club play their home games at Dean Court?

69. Which ground holds the record for the highest crowd in a European Cup final?

70. At which Stadium was the record for the smallest League Cup attendance at a top division ground set in 1992?

71. Which ground holds the record for the highest crowd at an FA Cup game other than the final, with 64,851?

72. Which club's ground is situated in Waterloo Road?

73. Disasters at which two grounds led to the Popplewell report being published?

74. When was the Charity Shield first played at Wembley?

75. At which ground was the 1970 FA Cup final replay held?

76. Where were the two semi-finals of the 1996 FA Cup played?

77. **where was the 1984 League Cup final replayed, when Liverpool beat Everton 1-0?**

78. At what ground was the 1981 League Cup replay held?

79. **At which ground did Nottingham Forest beat Liverpool in the 1978 League Cup final replay?**

80. At which two grounds did the two 1977 League Cup final replays occur?

81. **Which ground holds the record for the highest attendance in the Vauxhall conference of 9,432 in 1988?**

82. What ground was named England's national stadium in 1996?

83. **Where do Northern Ireland play their home internationals?**

84. At which ground did North Korea beat Italy in the 1966 World Cup?

85. **Which is Britain's most southwesterly League ground?**

86. Which club have moved ground 14 times since 1885?

87. **Which ground saw the first synthetic pitch in the British League?**

88. Which club started the 1997-98 season at the Britannia Stadium?

89. **Which Premiership club's stadium was used as a rifle range during World War One?**

90. Which club spent the first 23 years of their existance playing at Cassio Road?

91. Which club was the first to try executive boxes in their Grant Stand in 1898?

92. To which club's stadium is Pokesdown railway station the nearest?

93. In which ground is there a Charlie Brown Stand?

94. Which ground holds the record for an abandoned match?

95. At which ground is there a Bath End?

96. At which ground is there a Cemetry End and a Manchester Road End?

97. Which club's stadium has a Canton Stand and a Grangetown End?

98. Which team moved out of their Sealand Road ground to move in with Macclesfield, and then moved out again to their current Deva Stadium?

99. Which ground has an M & B Stand?

100. What is the name of Crewe Alexandra's stadium?

101. Which ground has an Arthur Wait Stand?

102. Norwood Junction is the nearest railway station to which ground?

103. Which team's stadium has an ASDA End with a grassy knoll?

104. Which stadium backs onto Gwladys Street and Bullens Road?

105. Which team's ground has a Pontoon End and a Findus Stand?

91. Celtic Park 92. Bournemouth **93. Bradford City's Valley Parade** 94. Newcastle's St James' Park **95. Bristol Rovers** 96. Gigg Lane **97. Cardiff City's Ninian Park** 98. Chester **99. Coventry - Highfield Road** 100. Gresty Road **101. Selhurst Park** 102. Selhurst Park **103. Doncaster Rovers' Belle Vue** 104. Goodison Park **105. Grimsby Town**

106. Which club play their home games at Edgar Street?

107. Which team play at Boothferry Park?

108. Which club has a Churchman's Stand and a Pioneer Stand?

109. On which Premiership ground do Hunslet Rugby League Club play?

110. South Bermondsey is the closest railway station to which club's stadium?

111. Which Norwich player scored the last goal in front of the Kop at Anfield before it became an all-seater stand?

112. Which stadium stands on the banks of the river Trent?

113. Which ground has the Lookers Stand and the Rochdale Road Stand?

114. Who scored the last two goals at Middlesborough's Ayesome Park before their move to the Riverside Stadium?

115. Which stadium has a Cuckoo Lane End and a London Road End?

116. Which club's stadium has a Glebe Road Terrace and a Moys End Terrace?

117. In which ground could you buy a fanzine called more Dead Wood Than The Mary Rose?

118. Which club's ground has a British Coal Opencast Stand?

119. Which ground has a South Africa Road Stand?

120. Which club plays their home games at the Spotland Stadium?

121. **Which club's home ground is called the McCain Stadium?**

122. Which ground has the Presto End?

123. **Which team play at Edgeley Park?**

124. At which stadium is there a Rous Stand and a Rookery End, which backs onto allotments?

125. **Which British club's ground became the first all-seater stadium in 1978?**

126. Which Scottish club's home ground is called Dens Park?

127. **Which British club play their home games at Tannadice Park?**

128. Which League ground hosted a semi-final in the 1997 Rugby League Silk Cut Challenge Cup?

129. **Which team play at Tynecastle Park?**

130. Who play their home games at Easter Road?

131. **Which club's home ground is called Fir Park?**

132. Which team play at Brockville Park, the smallest League pitch in Scotland?

133. **Which Scottish team play in a stadium designed for the 1970 Commonwealth Games?**

134. Wales have played every home game since 1921 in Cardiff, Wrexham and Swansea apart from one, in 1977. Where was this played?

135. **What is the most common name of a terrace/stand at British Football grounds?**

121. **Scarborough** 122. Hillsborough 123. **Stockport** 124. Watford's Vicarage Road 125. **Aberdeen's Pittodrie Stadium** 126. Dundee 127. **Dundee United** 128. The McAlpine Stadium 129. **Heart of Midlothian** 130. Hibernian 131. **Motherwell** 132. Falkirk 133. **Meadowbank Thistle** 134. Anfield 135. Spion Kop

Name........

1. The Wimbledon team that won the 1988 FA Cup Final.

2. England's side for the Euro '96 semi-final clash with Germany.

3. The Manchester United side who played Borussia Dortmund in the European Cup semi-final, first leg in 1997.

4. England's 1996 World Cup Final side.

5. The Arsenal side that clinched 'the double' when they beat Liverpool in the 1971 FA Cup Final.

6. The Everton side that beat Rapid Vienna in the 1985 European Cup-Winners' Cup Final.

7. The Arsenal team that beat Parma in the 1994 European Cup-Winners' Cup Final.

8. The Crystal Palace side that beat Liverpool in the 1990 FA Cup semi-final.

9. The Luton side that won the 1988 League Cup Final.

10. Scotland's Euro '96 side that played against England at Wembley.

11. **Liverpool's side that won the 1984 European Cup Final.**

12. The Ipswich side that won 3-0 at Portman Road in the 1981 Uefa Cup Final, first leg.

13. **The Celtic side that won the European Cup in 1967.**

14. Newcastle's team that lost 4-3 to Liverpool in the 1995-96 season.

15. **The Norwich City side that beat Bayern Munich 2-1 in the Uefa Cup, first leg in 1993-94.**

16. The Republic of Ireland side that beat England in the 1988 European Championship.

17. **The Nottingham Forest side that played the re-arranged FA Cup semi-final in 1989.**

18. Blackburn's team that beat Norwich City 7-1 in the 1992-93 season.

19. **The Everton side that escaped relegation by beating Wimbledon 3-2 in 1994.**

20. The Arsenal side that beat Liverpool 2-0 at Anfield to win the 1989 League Championship.

Merson (Hayes)

Winterburn, Thomas, O'Leary, Adams, Rocastle, Richardson, Smith, Bould (Groves), **Watson, Stuart, Horne, Cottee, Rideout, Limpar. 20. Lukic,** Dixon, (Wilcox), Addins, Shearer, Wegerle. **19. Southall, Snodin, Ablett, Unsworth,** Mimms, Brown, Wright, Sherwood, Hendry, Moran (Marker), Cowans, Ripley **Hodge, Gaynor (Starbuck), Webb, Clough, Chapman, Parker (Glover). 18.** Stapleton (Quinn), Galvin (Sheedy). **17. Sutton, Laws, Pearce, Walker, Wilson,** Bonner, Morris, Hughton, McCarthy, Moran, Whelan, McGrath, Houghton, Aldridge. **Newman, Bowen, Crook, Goss, Fox, Sutton, Robins (Sutch), Prior. 16.** Beardsley, Ginola, Asprilla, Ferdinand. **15. Gunn, Culverhouse, Butterworth,** Auld, Lennox. **14.** Smicek, Beresford, Howey (Peacock), Albert, Watson, Batty, Lee, **Craig, Gemmell, Murdoch, McNeill, Clark, Johnstone, Wallace, Chalmers,** Thijssen, Osman, Butcher, Wark, Muhren, Mariner, Brazil, Gates. **13. Simpson,** (Robinson), Lee, **Rush, Johnston (Nicol), Souness. 12.** Cooper, Mills, McCall, **11. Grobbelaar, Neal, Kennedy, Lawrenson, Whelan, Hansen, Dalglish**

21. **Nottingham Forest's 1979 European Cup Final team.**

22. Coventry's side that beat Tottenham in the 1987 FA Cup Final.

23. **The Republic of Ireland side that beat Italy in the 1994 World Cup.**

24. The Liverpool side that beat Crystal Palace 9-0 in the 1989-90 season.

25. **Dundee United's side that beat Rangers in the 1994 Scottish Cup Final.**

26. The England side that beat Cameroon in the 1990 World Cup.

27. **Scotland's team that beat Holland in the 1978 World Cup.**

28. The Wales team that beat West Germany in an European Championship qualifier in 1991.

29. **The Leeds side that lost to Sunderland in the 1973 FA Cup Final.**

30. Oxford United's team that won the 1986 League Cup Final.

21. Shilton, Anderson, Clark, McGovern, Lloyd, Burns, Francis, Bowyer, Birtles, Woodcock, Robertson. **22.** Ogrizovic, Phillips, Downs, McGrath, Kilcline (Rodger), Peake, Bennett, Gynn, Regis, Houchen, Pickering. **23.** Bonner, Irwin, Babb, McGrath, Phelan, Houghton (McAteer), Sheridan, Keane, Townsend, Staunton, Coyne (Aldridge) **24.** Grobbelaar, Hysen, Burrows, Nicol, Whelan, Hansen, Beardsley (Aldridge), Rush, Barnes, McMahon, Gillespie (Molby). **25.** Van de Kamp, Cleland, Malpas, McInally, Petric, Welsh, Bowman, Hannah, Nicholas, Saunders (Speed), Rush, Hughes, Horne. **26.** Shilton, Parker, Walker, Wright, Butcher (Steven), Pearce, Waddle, Gascoigne, Platt, Barnes (Beardsley), Lineker. **27.** Rough, Kennedy, Donachie, Rioch, Forsyth, Buchan, Dalglish, Hartford, Jordan, Gemmill, Souness. **28.** Southall, Phillips, Melville, Bodin, Aizlewood, Ratcliffe, Nicholas, Saunders (Speed), Rush, Hughes, Horne. **29.** Harvey, Reaney, Cherry, Bremner, Madeley, Hunter, Lorimer, Clarke, Jones, Giles, Gray (Yorath). **30.** Judge, Langan, Trewick, Phillips, Briggs, Shotton, Houghton, Aldridge, Charles, Hebberd, Brock.

1. **Which two British players have played in European Cup Finals for more than one club?**

2. Who were the last two men to manage English clubs to European Cup success?

3. **Who scored Manchester United's goal at Old Trafford against Rotor Volgograd in the Uefa Cup in 1995?**

4. Who is the last person to score in an European Final for a British club?

5. **Name the five clubs that have won the European Cup at Wembley?**

6. Who were Nottingham Forest's first opponents in the European Cup?

7. **Who is the only British manager to have won the European Cup-Winners Cup with different clubs?**

8. Which team did Manchester United play in their first European Cup tie?

9. **Which club did Manchester United defeat to reach the 1968 European Cup Final?**

10. Which team did Chelsea beat in the final to win the European Cup-Winners Cup in 1971?

11. **Which other English team did Chelsea beat in the semi-finals to reach the 1971 European Cup-Winners Cup Final?**

12. The 1971 European Cup-Winners Cup Final went to a replay. Who scored in both games of the Final?

13. **Which British club beat AC Milan on a toss of a coin in the Inter-Cities Fairs Cup third round in 1966?**

14. Which two present day managers played in that tie?

15. **Which English club recorded a 21-0 aggregate score over Luxembourg club Jeunesse Hautcharage in the European Cup-Winners Cup in 1971-72?**

1. **Kevin Keegan (Liverpool & Hamburg), Frank Gray (Leeds &** Hartson 5. **AC Milan, Manchester United, Ajax, Liverpool, Barcelona** 6. **Nottingham Forest)** 2. Joe Fagan, Tony Barton 3. **Peter Schmeichel** 4. John Liverpool 7. **Alex Fergsuon (Aberdeen & Manchester United)** 8. Anderlecht 9. **Real Madrid** 10. Real Madrid 11. **Manchester City** 12. Peter Osgood 13. Chelsea 14. Terry Venables & George Graham 15. **Chelsea**

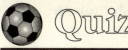
16. Who were the first British club to play in a European Cup Final?

17. Which Yugoslavian side knocked Arsenal out of the 1979 Uefa Cup?

18. Who did Arsenal beat to reach the 1980 European Cup-Winners Cup Final?

19. Who scored the winning goal in the second leg of that game?

20. Arsenal were beaten in the 1980 European Cup-Winners Final on penalties. By which Spanish side?

21. Which England international missed the decisive penalty?

22. Which Russian club won 5-2 at Highbury to knock Arsenal out of the 1982-83 Uefa Cup?

23. Which club knocked Arsenal out of the 1972 European Cup on their way to winning to the trophy?

24. Which English club beat Anderlecht 4-3 on aggregate to win the 1970 Inter-Cities Fairs Cup?

25. When they defended the Cup the following season, which German club beat them in the fourth round?

26. In what season did Arsenal make their first appearance in European competition?

27. Who were they beaten by in the second round?

28. Who did Arsenal beat to win the 1994 European Cup-Winners Cup?

29. Who scored the only goal?

30. In defence of their title, Arsenal lost in the 1995 European Cup-Winners Cup Final. Which Spanish side beat them?

Quiz 23 British Clubs In Europe

31. **Where was that Final played?**

32. Which former Tottenham player scored the winning goal in that Final with a 40-yard lob over David Seaman?

33. **Which England international missed the 1994 European Cup-Winners Cup Final through suspension?**

34. Who won the European Cup with Juventus before moving to England?

35. **Who were the first English winners of the European Cup-Winners Cup?**

36. Which English club reached the European Cup semi-final in their first season of the competition?

37. **Liverpool collected their first European trophy when they won the 1966 European Cup-Winners Cup. Who did they beat in the Final?**

38. Who scored the only goal?

39. **Which German club were beaten 8-0 by Liverpool in the 1967-68 Inter-Cities Fairs Cup at Anfield?**

40. Which English club beat Irish club Dundalk 14-0 on aggregate in the 1969-70 Inter-Cities Fairs Cup?

41. **Which two English clubs contested one of the 1971 Inter-Cities Fairs Cup semi-finals?**

42. And who won through to the Final?

43. **Liverpool won the 1973 Uefa Cup by beating which German side over two legs?**

44. Despite losing the second leg 2-0, Liverpool won the 1973 Uefa Cup final 3-2 on aggregate. Who scored Liverpool's goals in the first leg?

45. **Who did Liverpool beat in the semi-finals of the that year?**

31. **Paris** 32. Nayim 33. **Ian Wright** 34. Gianluca Vialli (Juventus) 35. **Tottenham** 36. Liverpool 37. **Borussia Dortmund** 38. Roger Hunt 39. **Munich 1860** 40. Liverpool 41. **Leeds and Liverpool** 42. Leeds 43. **Borussia Moenchengladbach** 44. Kevin Keegan (2), Larry Lloyd 45. **Tottenham**

Quiz 23 — British Clubs In Europe

46. In the 1974-75 European Cup-Winners Cup first round, Liverpool beat Stromsgodset 11-0 at Anfield. How many different players were on the scoresheet?

47. **Liverpool beat Belgian side FC Bruges twice in three years in European Finals. What competitions?**

48. How many years did Liverpool win consecutive European Finals in the mid-1970's?

49. **Kevin Keegan made his final appearance for Liverpool in the 1977 European Cup Final. Did he score?**

50. What were the similiarities between Liverpool's European Cup success in 1977 and 1984?

51. **Where did Liverpool win the 1978 European Cup Final?**

52. Who scored Liverpool's winning goal?

53. **Which team did Liverpool meet in successive European Cup seasons in the last-1970's?**

54. Before the ban on English clubs, how many successive seasons did Liverpool play in the European Cup?

55. **Which Scottish club were beaten 5-0 on aggregate by Liverpool in the 1980-81 European Cup?**

56. Was it Ray Kennedy or Alan Kennedy who scored the only goal in Liverpool's 1981 European Cup Final success?

57. **Who did Liverpool beat in that Final?**

58. Who knocked the reigning champions, Liverpool, out of the 1982 European Cup?

59. **Who scored Liverpool's goal in open-play in the 1984 European Cup Final?**

60. Name the four Liverpool players who scored from the spot in the 1984 European Cup Final penalty shoot-out?

46. Nine 47. **Uefa Cup (1976), European Cup (1978)** 48. Three (1976,1977,1978) 49. **No** 50. Both Finals were played in Rome 51. **Wembley** 52. Kenny Dalglish 53. **Borussia Moenchengladbach** 54. Nine 55. **Aberdeen** 56. Alan Kennedy 57. **Real Madrid** 58. CSKA Sofia 59. **Phil Neal** 60. Phil Neal, Ian Rush, Graeme Souness & Alan Kennedy

61. The 1985 European Cup Final between Liverpool and Juventus was marred by crowd violence at the Heysel stadium. But who scored the only goal for the Italian club?

62. Who resigned as Liverpool manager after that game?

63. How did Liverpool beat Cologne in the 1965 European Cup quarter-final?

64. Who scored West Ham's two goals in their 1965 European Cup-Winners Cup Final success?

65. Where was that Final played?

66. How many British clubs have competed in European Finals at Wembley?

67. What round did West Ham reach in the European Cup-Winners Cup in 1980-81?

68. Who were Manchester United beaten by in the group stages of the 1996-97 Champions League?

69. Who beat West Ham in the 1976 European Cup-Winners Cup Final?

70. Who did Everton beat over two legs in the semi-finals of the 1985 European Cup-Winners Cup?

71. Everton beat which Austrian club in the European Cup-Winners Cup Final of 1985?

72. Who scored Everton's goals in that Final victory?

73. Which Scottish side beat Everton in the 1962-63 Uefa Cup?

74. Which English club did Inter Milan beat on their way to winning the 1964 European Cup?

75. Who captained Everton to their European Cup-Winners Cup success in 1985?

61. Michel Platini **62.** Joe Fagan **63.** On a toss of a coin **64.** Alan Sealey **65.** Wembley **66.** Three. Manchester United, Liverpool & West Ham **67.** Quarter-finals **68.** Juventus (twice) and Fenerbahce **69.** Anderlecht **70.** Bayern Munich **71.** Rapid Vienna **72.** Andy Gray, Trevor Steven & Kevin Sheedy **73.** Dunfermline **74.** Everton **75.** Kevin Ratcliffe

76. Which England international goalkeeper had to be taken off after only eight minutes of the 1982 European Cup Final?

77. Which youngster replaced him?

78. Manchester United reached the semi-finals of the European Cup in 1957. Which legendary team beat them?

79. Manchester United were beaten the following year again in the semi-finals. Who inflicted defeat this time?

80. When Manchester United beat Benfica to win the European Cup in 1968, who scored twice for United?

81. On defending the European Cup in 1969, Manchester United were beaten in the semi-finals. By who?

82. Which two English teams met in the European Cup-Winners Cup second round in the 1963-64 season?

83. Who won the tie?

84. Which Italian club beat Manchester United in the 1984 European Cup-Winners Cup semi-final?

85. Who scored Manchester United's other two goals in the 1968 European Cup Final?

86. Who scored for Celtic in their memorable European Cup Final success in 1967?

87. Who was Celtic's victorious captain on that day?

88. Which Manchester United striker missed the 1968 European Cup Final through injury?

89. Which former European Footballer of the Year played against Manchester United in the 1968 European Cup Final?

90. Who were nicknamed 'The Lisbon Lions' after their European Cup success?

91. How many European Cup Finals have Celtic appeared in?

92. Who has scored twice in European Cup Finals for Celtic?

93. Which Dutch side beat Celtic in the European Cup Final of 1970?

94. Which English side were beaten by Bayern Munich in an European Cup Final?

95. Which brothers played in the Leeds side that played in the 1975 European Cup Final?

96. Which club played in five European Cup Finals in the 1960's, winning twice?

97. Which Dutchman won the Uefa Cup in 1981 for Ipswich and had a brother that won the European Cup in 1972?

98. Which Spainsh club did Leeds beat to reach the 1975 European Cup Final?

99. Which former Wales manager played for Leeds in the 1975 European Cup Final?

100. Which English side beat Real Madrid 4-1 in the European Cup second round first leg, only to be beaten 6-5 on aggregate?

101. Who scored a hat-trick in that first leg, and also scored in the return?

102. Which English side won the European Cup at the first attempt?

103. Who scored the winning away goal for Nottingham Forest against Cologne in the 1979 European Cup semi-final, second leg?

104. Which former Nottingham Forest manager played for the club in the 1979 European Cup Final?

105. Who scored the only goal for Nottingham Forest in the 1979 European Cup Final?

106. Which Brazilian, who would later play in the Premiership, scored for Genoa against Liverpool in the 1992 Uefa Cup?

107. **Who did Nottingham Forest beat in the 1980 European Cup semi-finals?**

108. Who scored the winning goal for Nottingham Forest in the 1980 European Cup Final?

109. **Which England captain played against Nottingham Forest in the 1980 European Cup Final?**

110. Which English club did Rangers beat in the European Cup-Winners Cup semi-final in 1961?

111. **Which Italian club beat Rangers in the 1961 European Cup-Winners Cup Final?**

112. What round did Scottish club Dunfermline reach in the 1962 European Cup-Winners Cup?

113. **Rangers lost to who in the 1963 European Cup-Winners Cup?**

114. Rangers reached the 1967 European Cup-Winners Cup Final. Who did they play?

115. **Which British club reached the European Cup-Winners Cup semi-final in 1968?**

116. Which Scottish team reached the semi-finals in the same competition a year later?

117. **Which English club won the European Cup-Winners Cup in 1970?**

118. Who were their scorers in the Final?

119. **Which Scottish club won the European Cup-Winners Cup in 1972?**

120. Who did they beat in the Final?

106. Branco **107. Ajax** 108. John Robertson **109. Kevin Keegan** 110. Wolves **111. Fiorentina** 112. Quarter-Finals **113. Tottenham** 114. Bayern Munich **115. Cardiff City** 116. Dunfermline **117. Manchester City** 118. Neil Young and Francis Lee (pen) **119. Rangers** 120. Dynamo Moscow

121. Leeds reached the European Cup-Winners Cup Final in 1973. Who beat them in the Final?

122. Which Irish team reached the 1974 European Cup-Winners Cup quarter-finals before being beaten by Borussia Moenchengladbach?

123. Who were England's representatives in the 1973-74 European Cup-Winners Cup?

124. Which Hungarian side knocked Liverpool out of the 1975 European Cup-Winners Cup on their way to the Final?

125. Who did West Ham beat in the 1976 European Cup-Winners Cup semi-final?

126. Who scored twice for West Ham in the second leg of that semi-final?

127. Who beat West Ham in the 1976 European Cup-Winners Cup Final?

128. Which English club did Anderlecht beat in the 1977 European Cup-Winners Cup quarter-finals?

129. Which English team beat Porto 5-2 in the second leg of the 1978 European Cup-Winners Cup second round, but still lost 6-5 on aggregate?

130. Which English side lost on away goals to Barcelona in the quarter-finals of the 1979 European Cup-Winners Cup?

131. Who played in European Cup-Winners Cup Finals for Chelsea and Arsenal?

132. Which British club played in consecutive Fairs Cup Finals in the 1960's?

133. Which British club were the first to reach an European club final?

134. Which three British clubs were in the 1966 Uefa Cup quarter-finals?

135. Leeds played in consecutive Fairs Cup Finals in the 1960's. Which years?

136. On reaching the two Finals, Leeds beat Scottish clubs in both semi-finals. Who were they?

137. Which European trophy did Newcastle win in 1969?

138. Which two English clubs contested the 1972 Uefa Cup Final?

139. Which Premiership manager played for Tottenham in the 1972 Uefa Cup Final?

140. Who beat Tottenham on away goals to reach the 1973 Uefa Cup Final?

141. Who beat Tottenham in the 1974 Uefa Cup Final?

142. Aston Villa were beaten by Barcelona in the Uefa Cup qaurter-finals in 1978. But who scored their consolation goal at the Nou Camp?

143. Which Midlands club reached the Uefa Cup quarter-finals in 1979?

144. Which two Ipswich players scored in both legs of the 1981 Uefa Cup Final?

145. Which English club lost in the 1959 European Cup first round?

146. Which English club did Barcelona beat 9-2 on aggregate in the 1960 European Cup?

147. What English team reached the quarter-finals of the European Cup in 1961?

148. Who was in goal for Manchester United when Barcelona beat them 4-0 in the Champions League in 1994-95?

149. Which other British club were beaten by Bayern Munich in the 1995-96 Uefa Cup?

150. Which club did Real Zaragoza beat to reach the 1995 European Cup-Winners Cup Final?

136. Kilmarnock and Dundee 137. **Fairs Cup** 138. Tottenham and Wolves 139. **Joe Kinnear** 140. Liverpool 141. **Feyenoord** 142. Brian Little 143. **W.B.A.** 144. John Wark and Frans Thijssen 145. **Wolves** 146. **Wolves** 147. Wolves 148. Gary Walsh 149. **Raith Rovers** 150. Chelsea

151. Who did Newcastle lose to in the second round of the 1995 Uefa Cup?

152. Which club of Swedish part-timers beat Blackburn in the first round of the 1994-95 Uefa Cup?

153. To qualify for the 1992-93 Champions League, the English champions faced the Scottish champions. Who won the tie?

154. What was the aggregate score?

155. Rangers missed out on qualifying for the European Cup Final of 1993 by one point in the group stage. Who topped the group?

156. Who scored twice for Manchester United in their 1991 European Cup-Winners Cup Final victory over Barcelona?

157. English clubs were allowed back into European competitions in 1990-91. Why did they not have a representative in the European Cup?

158. Which Premiership striker played in the 1992 European Cup Final?

159. Who did Arsenal lose to in the European Cup second round in 1991-92?

160. How many group matches did Blackburn win in the 1995-96 Champions League?

161. Who scored a hat-trick for Blackburn in the 1995-96 Champions League?

162. Which German, Romanian and Italian side were in Rangers' Champions League group in 1995-96?

163. Who beat Celtic on their way to winning the 1996 European Cup-Winners Cup?

164. Nottingham Forest lost in the Uefa Cup quarter-finals in 1996 to Bayern Munich 7-2 on aggregate. What was the score after the first leg in Germany?

165. Who, in 1993-94, became the first British side to beat Bayern Munich in an European competition in Germany?

---

151. **Athletico Bilbao** 152. Trelleborgs 153. **Rangers** 154. 4-2 155. **Marseille**
156. Mark Hughes 157. **Because Liverpool were banned for another three years** 158. Gianluca Vialli (Sampdoria) 159. **Benfica** 160. One 161. **Mike Newell**
162. Borussia Dortmund, Steaua Bucharest and Juventus 163. **Paris St Germain**
164. 2-1 to Munich 165. **Norwich City**

166. Who scored the two goals when Norwich beat Bayern Munich in the Uefa Cup second round, first leg in 1993-94?

167. Who scored both Inter Milan goals in their 2-0 aggregate victory over Norwich in 1994 Uefa Cup third round?

168. Which Italian club did Arsenal beat on their way to the 1994 European Cup-Winners Cup Final?

169. Who did Manchester United lose to on away goals in the 1994 European Cup second round?

170. Rangers also lost on away goals in the second round of the 1994 European Cup. Who to?

171. When was the last European final to be played at Wembley?

172. Manchester United's lost their first Champions League match of the 1996-97 season. Who to?

173. Who scored the only goal?

174. Who did Arsenal lose to in the first round of the 1996-97 Uefa Cup?

175. Who were the only two British clubs to reach the second round of the Uefa Cup in 1996-97?

176. Who scored Manchester United's first goal in the 1996-97 Champions League?

177. Which former West Ham forward scored twice for Ajax in Rangers' 4-1 Champions League defeat in 1996-97?

178. Who was sent-off for Rangers in that match?

179. What was the score in Liverpool's second round, second leg tie against FC Sion?

180. Who knocked Newcastle out of the 1997 Uefa Cup?

Quiz 24 — Moonlighting Footballers

1. **'Fever Pitch' is a book on one fan's obsession with his favourite football club. Which Premiership club does he support?**

2. Which famous actor narrated 'Hero', the official film of the 1986 World Cup?

3. **Which former England international appeared in the film 'When Saturday Comes'?**

4. What was the name of the award winning television drama about the Hillsborough disaster?

5. **Which club was the subject of the documentary 'Yours for a Fiver'?**

6. What was the title of the Cutting Edge television documentary that chronicled Graham Taylor as England manager?

7. **Which international manager wrote the television show 'Hazel'?**

8. Which England international had a hit record with 'Do The Right Thing'?

9. **Which footballers have appeared in adverts for Brut aftershave?**

10. Glenn Hoddle and Chris Waddle had a hit song when they were playing at Tottenham. What was the title of the song?

11. **Ruud Gullit used to be a member of a band. What music did they play?**

12. Which Premiership player appeared in the film 'Le Bonheur Est Dans Le Pre'?

13. **Name the title of the famous play and television programme An Evening with ....**

14. Which Nottingham Forest striker is a singer in a band?

15. **Who wrote the book 'Fever Pitch'?**

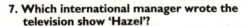

1. **Arsenal** 2. Michael Caine 3. **Tony Currie** 4. 'Hillsborough' 5. **Leyton Orient** 6. ' The Impossible Job' 7. **Terry Venables** 8. Ian Wright 9. **Kevin Keegan and Paul Gascoigne** 10. Diamond Lights 11. **Reggae** 12. Eric Cantona 13. **Gary Lineker** 14. Paul McGregor 15. **Nick Hornby**

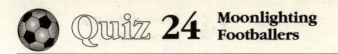

16. Which famous footballer orchestrated the football action in 'Escape to Victory'?

17. Which former England international has advertised Walkers Crisps?

18. The war film 'Escape to Victory' featured a football match between Allied prisoners and West Germany. Who was the manager of the Allies?

19. Which former England captain was in the Allies team in 'Escape to Victory'?

20. What position did Sylvester Stallone's play in 'Escape to Victory'?

21. Which England international writes a weekly article for The Times?

22. Which Croatian footballer had his own column in the Daily Telegraph during Euro '96?

23. Which former Arsenal and England striker occasionally writes for the Daily Telegraph?

24. Which two former Scotland internationals write for The Express?

25. Which England goalscorer wrote for the Observer?

26. Which former England international has a column in the football magazine 'Four-Four-Two'?

27. Which television summariser appeared on a Littlewoods Pools advert in 1997?

28. Which two Premiership players featured in a Nike advertisment in 1996?

29. Which England international has appeared in advertisments for sportswear Adidas?

30. Which Premiership footballer appeared in television adverts for Eurostar?

31. Which Manchester United and Manchester City players became partners in two lady boutiques?

32. Which two players from England's 1966 World Cup squad went into partnership in a football kit company?

33. Which team sung the number one hit 'Back Home' in 1970?

34. Tottenham's 1981 FA Cup Final song reached number five in the charts. Whose dream were they singing about?

35. Which nation's World Cup song was titled 'Easy, Easy'?

36. 'Blue is the Colour' was a number five hit for which club in February 1972?

37. Which England goalkeeper worked as a deck-chair assistant before turning professional?

38. Which FA Cup winning manager was a clerk in an education office before he took up football?

39. Which England 1966 World Cup star sung a version of 'You'll Never Walk Alone', but it never reached the charts?

40. Which former England captain had a number 31 hit with 'Head Over Heels in Love' in June 1979?

41. Which Spanish singer was once a Real Madrid goalkeeper?

42. Which Tottenham and Wales striker invested in two butchers shops after finishing his career?

43. Which French footballer appeared in a Renault advertisement?

44. Which television commentator supplied the voice-over for that advert?

45. Highbury was at the centre of which movie?

31. George Best and Mike Summerbee 32. Geoff Hurst and Jimmy Greaves 33. England's World Cup squad 34. Ossie's (Ardiles) 35. Scotland in 1974 36. Chelsea 37. Ray Clemence 38. Lawrie McMenemy 39. Jack Charlton 40. Kevin Keegan 41. Julio Iglesias 42. Cliff Jones 43. David Ginola 44. John Motson 45. The Arsenal Stadium Murder Mystery

1. **In which year did Middlesbrough make Sunderland's Alf Common the first £1,000 player, 1903, 1904, 1905?**

2. Who made the first five-figure move in 1928?

3. **Who left Tranmere for £3,000 in 1925 and three years later set a goalscoring record which has stood for 70 years?**

4. In 1996 Queens Park Rangers manager Ray Wilkins put a valuation on winger Trevor Sinclair. Was it £8million, £9.5million, £10m?

5. **Which two internationals moved from Derby County to Liverpool in July 1991 for a combined total of over £5million?**

6. What sum did Lazio ORIGINALLY offer Tottenham for Paul Gascoigne in 1991?

7. **How much did Tottenham eventually receive for Gascoigne?**

8. Who was Wimbledon's first £1million signing in 1996?

9. **At the start of the 1996-7 season who was Rochdale's most expensive buy?**

10. What was the name of the Norwegian agent at the centre of the "bung" transfer scandal in 1996?

11. **Denis Law became Britain's first £100,000 player in 1962. From which club did Manchester United buy him?**

12. In 1968 the world transfer record was shattered by a £440,000 Italian internal move. Name the player and clubs involved.

13. **Who was involved in Britain's first £200,000 transfer?**

14. In 1973 Johan Cruyff was involved in the first £1million transfer. Which two clubs were involved?

15. **When Kevin Keegan left Liverpool in 1977 how much did Hamburg pay for his services?**

16. Also in 1977 the record fee for a transfer between British clubs soared to £440,000. Name the player and clubs involved.

17. **How much did Kevin Keegan spend in his first four years as Newcastle manager?**

18. In February 1996 Coventry signed a defender and a forward for a combined £3.1million. Who were they?

19. **Which two foreign players were prevented from switching Premiership clubs when the DoE initially refused new work permits in February 1996?**

20. Which clubs did the pair eventually join?

21. **In which year was Britain's first £1million transfer?**

22. Who was the player involved, the clubs and the fee?

23. **At the start of the 1996-97 season only one British player had been transferred for more than £5million on three occasions. Name him.**

24. Name the first 10 British players to cost £5million or more.

25. **Which Premiership club had three players costing £5million or more on their books at the start of the 1996-97 season?**

26. How much did Paul Gascoigne cost Rangers when he moved from Lazio in July 1995?

27. **What was the fee when striker Tony Cascarino joined Gillingham from non-League Crockenhill in 1982?**

28. How much did Cascarino cost Aston Villa when he moved from Millwall in March 1990?

29. **Why was Jimmy Greaves fee settled at £99,999 when he joined Tottenham from AC Milan in December 1961?**

30. Which Scottish club shattered the £2,000 barrier for West Ham's Syd Puddefoot in February 1922?

16. Kenny Dalglish - Celtic to Liverpool 17. **£44m** 18. Liam Daish (Birmingham) and Eoin Jess (Aberdeen) 19. **Ilie Dumitrescu and Marc Hottger** 20. West Ham and Everton 21. **1979** 22. Trevor Francis - Birmingham to Nottingham Forest, £1.18m 23. **David Platt** 24. Stan Collymore, Andy Cole, David Platt, Paul Ince, Les Ferdinand, Paul Gascoigne, Nick Barmby, Trevor Steven, Chris Sutton and Alan Shearer 25. **Newcastle (Alan Shearer, Faustino Asprilla and Les Ferdinand** 26. £4.3m 27. **A set of tracksuits** 28. £1.5m 29. **Manager Bill Nicholson** thought Greaves' form would suffer if he was tagged the first £100,000 player 30. **Falkirk**

31. Denis Law's record-breaking £100,000 move to Torino in June 1961 was followed by another 13 months later. What was the buying club and his new valuation?

32. Who made English football's first big-money move to Italy and for how much?

33. Which England striker moved from Chelsea to Notts County for £20,000 in November 1947?

34. Name the player who scored in the first Wembley FA Cup Final and joined Arsenal in October 1928 for a record £10,890.

35. The biggest immediate post-war transfer fee went North of the border. Which club collected £15,000 when Billy Steel moved to Derby in September 1947?

36. The "clown prince" of football transferred from Newcastle to Sunderland in February 1948 for £20,500. Who was he?

37. Name the player and the clubs involved in the first £150,000 English transfer?

38. Which Welsh international moved from Leeds to Juventus for £65,000 in April 1957?

39. Which club was known as the "Bank of England club" when knocked out of the FA Cup by non-League Yeovil in 1949?

40. A member of England's world cup winning squad was involved in a big transfer within weeks of the 1966 triumph. Name the player, the clubs and the fee involved.

41. Before Alan Shearer's £15million move from Blackburn to Newcastle, which Italian was the world's most expensive player?

42. In which month is the annual transfer deadline?

43. Name the subject of the world's first £1million transfer and the clubs involved .

44. Who became the most expensive player in Britain when he moved from Middlesbrough to West Bromwich Albion in January 1979 for £516,000?

45. In 1992 AC Milan spent £23,000 on two players within a month. Who were they?

46. Beazer Homes League club Rushden and Diamonds shattered the record fee for a non-League player in March 1996. Who was the player, the fee and the other club involved?

47. **Which club did Welsh international Dean Saunders join for £1.5million when he left Aston Villa in July 1995?**

48. Diego Maradona left Napoli for which club in a £4million deal in September 1992?

49. **From which club did Newcastle purchase striker Faustino Asprilla for £6.7million in February 1996?**

50. Just before the start of the 1995-96 season Wigan signed Spaniards Jesus Seba, Roberto Martinez and Isidro Diaz. By what name were they collectively known?

51. **Which club did Jurgen Klinsmann leave to join Tottenham?**

52. Who moved to Barcelona from Manchester United in May 1986 for £2.3m?

53. **Who moved from Manchester United to AC Milan for £1.5m in 1984?**

54. Who moved to Liverpool from Newcastle for £1.9m in July 1987?

55. **Which French club did Clive Allen join from Tottenham?**

56. From which club did Manchester United buy Peter Schmeichel?

57. **How did James Oakes come to play for both clubs in the same League fixture in the 1932-33 season?**

58. How much did Ruel Fox cost Tottenham when he joined from Newcastle in October 1995?

59. **Also in 1995 Andy Cole's transfer from Newcastle to Manchester United set a new British record. How much?**

60. Which player moved from Manchester United to Newcastle as part of the Andy Cole deal?

46. Carl Alford from Kettering for £85,000 47. **Galatasaray** 48. Seville 49. **Parma** 50. "The three Amigos" 51. **Monaco** 52. Mark Hughes 53. **Ray Wilkins** 54. Peter Beardsley 55. **Bordeaux** 56. Brondby 57. **He played for Port Vale against Charlton on Boxing Day 1932 when the game was abandoned. By the time of the re-arranged match Oakes had been transferred to Charlton and played against his old club** 58. £4.2m 59. **£7m** 60. Keith Gillespie

61. **Another record British transfer was set when striker Duncan Ferguson moved from Dundee United to Rangers in 1993. How much was the fee?**

62. **The record went a year later when Chris Sutton moved from Norwich to Blackburn for how much?**

63. **In 1996 Manchester United were found guilty of an illegal approach to the teenaged son of a League club manager. Who was he?**

64. Striker Marco Gabbiadini has cost which two clubs over one million pounds?

65. **What was the fee when Ray Wilkins left Paris St. Germain for Rangers in November 1987?**

66. Which Belgian defender did Newcastle sign in August 1994?

67. **How much did Phillipe Albert cost Newcastle?**

68. Andy Cole's £7m signing by Manchester United in 1995 set a new British record fee. Who was the second most expensive player on the Old Trafford books at the time?

69. **Name the four French clubs Eric Cantona played for before his £900,000 move to Leeds in 1992?**

70. Gary Pallister became the most expensive defender in Britain when he joined Manchester United from Middlesbrough in 1989 for how much?

71. **How much did Ruud Gullit cost Chelsea when he arrived as a player in August 1995?**

72. Who cost Blackburn £2.7m from Sheffield Wednesday in August 1993?

73. **How much did Crystal Palace collect when Ian Wright went to Arsenal in September 1991?**

74. In 1979 West Bromwich Albion sold a forward to Real Madrid. Who was he and what was the fee?

75. **Which player was paraded around the Baseball Ground as Derby County's latest big signing in 1972 - only to change his mind and join Manchester United instead?**

Ian Storey-Moore

61. £4m 62. £5m 63. Matthew Wicks 64. Crystal Palace and Derby County 65. £250,000 66. Phillipe Albert 67. £2.65m 68. Roy Keane (£3.75m) 69. Auxerre, Marseille, Bordeaux and Nimes 70. £2.3m 71. Nothing - Free transfer from Sampdoria 72. Paul Warhurst 73. £2.5m 74. Laurie Cunningham - £995,000 75.

Quiz 25 — Britain's Biggest Transfers

76. Which forward was sold for a Huddersfield record £2.7million to Sheffield Wednesday in 1996?

77. Who became Britain's most expensive teenager when he moved from Charlton to Leeds in July 1996?

78 How much did Bowyer cost?

79. Who joined a London club in a £1million-plus deal but never played a first-team game for them?

80. Which other London club did he join after just three weeks?

81. Chris Armstrong left Crystal Palace for Tottenham in June 1995 for how much?

82. Ian Rush left Liverpool in 1987 for which club and how much was the fee?

83. How much did Rush cost Liverpool when he returned in August 1988?

84. When Richard Gough left Tottenham for Rangers in October 1987 the £1.5million deal set three records. What were they?

85. At which English club did Richard Gough start his playing career?

86. Tottenham shattered the British record fee when they signed winger Cliff Jones from Swansea in February 1985. How much did he cost?

87. Which Staffordshire-born player shattered the British transfer record twice in a year at the end of the 1960's while yet to be capped by his country?

88. Which clubs and fees were involved in Clarke's moves?

89. Which striker moved from Birmingham to Everton for £350,000 in February 1974?

90. From which club did Welsh international midfielder Peter Nicholas join Chelsea in August 1988?

91. What was the fee?

92. Brighton set a new fee record for a non-League player when they forked out £115,000 in September 1988. Who was the player and the other club involved?

93. A week later Brighton signed another Barnet player for an identical sum. Who was he?

94. Which record was set by David Leworthy when he moved from Farnborough to Dover in August 1993 for £30,000?

95. Who was the first £1million British goalkeeper?

96. Which clubs were involved in Martyn's November 1989 move?

97. Two years later five more goalkeepers had moved on in Britain for £1million or more. Who were they?

98. Back in 1964 the record fee for a British goalkeeper was collected by Crystal Palace from Coventry. Who was the goalkeeper and what was the fee involved?

99. Manchester United paid record fees for goakeepers in 1966 and 1988. Who were they?

100. Queens Park Rangers collected record fees for goalkeepers in 1979 and 1990. Who were they?

101. Which goalkeeper was transferred twice for a record £50,000 within five months of the year 1966?

102. Name the clubs involved in Stepney's moves.

103. Which two records did Alexei Mikhailichenko's transfer from Sampdoria to Rangers set in 1991?

104. How much was the fee?

105. In August 1991 three players left Liverpool for around £1million each. Who were they?

104. £2m 105. Steve Staunton, Peter Beardsley, Gary Gillespie

United 103. Record fee for a Scottish club, most expensive foreign import
David Seaman. John Lukic, Tony Coton, Andy Goram and Chris Woods 98.
Bill Glazier - £35,000 99. Iex Stepney and Jim Leighton 100. Phil Parkes and
David Seaman. 101. Alex Stepney 102. Millwall-Chelsea, Chelsea-Manchester

non-league clubs 95. Nigel Martyn 96. Bristol Rovers and Crystal palace 97.
91. £350,000 92. Nicky Bissett 93. Robert Codner 94. The highest fee between

1. **Which former Manchester City manager said: "I'm not a believer in luck, although I do believe you need it"?**

2. Which manager said of his side's FA Cup chances: "I honestly believe we can go all the way to Wembley.....unless someone knocks us out"?

3. **Which former manager stated: "I promise results, not promises"?**

4. Which former Aston Villa manager said of chairman Doug Ellis: "He said he was right behind me, so I told him I'd rather have him in front of me where I could see him"?

5. **Which legendary manager once said: "Mind, I've been here during the bad times too. One year we finished second"?**

6. Which charismatic manager said: "John Bond has blackened my name with his insinuations about the private lives of football managers. Both my wives are upset."

7. **Who said of women in football: "Women should be in the kitchen, the discotheque and the boutique, but not in football"?**

8. Which former QPR and England striker once said: "If I had a choice of a night with Raquel Welch or going to a betting shop, I'd choose the betting shop"?

9. **Which former manager said: "The ideal board of directors should be made up of three men - two dead and one dying"?**

10. Which former manager said: "Football hooligans? Well, there are ninety-two club chairmen, for a start"?

Quiz 26 **Who Said ?**

11. Which former England striker said of Kenny Dalglish: "He has about as much personality as a tennis racket"?

12. Who said: "Trevor Brooking floats like a butterfly, and stings like one too"?

13. Which commentator said: "Lukic saved with his foot which is all part of the goalkeeper's arm"?

14. Which former manager said of Ray Wilkins: "He can't run, he can't tackle and he can't head the ball. The only time he goes forward is to toss the coin"?

15. What television commentator said: "The game is balanced in Arsenal's favour"?

16. Which commentator stated: "With the very last kick of the game, Bobby McDonald scored with a header"?

17. Which international manager once said: "If history is going to repeat itself, I should think we can expect the same thing again"?

18. Which former England manager said: "The first ninety minutes are the most important"?

19. Which TV commentator said: "The European Cup is seventeen pounds of silver and it's worth it's weight in gold"?

20. Which international striker said: "Moving from Wales to Italy is like going to a different country"?

21. **Which commentator said: "The ball has broken 50-50 for Keegan"?**

22. Which England international remarked: "I never predict anything and I never will do"?

23. **Which former Liverpool manager said: "Without picking out anyone in particular, I thought Mark Wright was tremendous"?**

24. Which former England captain once said: "If you never concede a goal, you're going to win more games than you lose"?

25. **Name the former Newcastle manager who said: "There's no job I've ever wanted. This is the only job in football I've ever wanted."**

26. Which international manager once said: "It may have just been going wide, but nevertheless it was a great shot on target"?

27. **Which radio commentator said: "Fifty-two thousand people here at Maine Road tonight, but my goodness me, it seems like fifty-thousand"?**

28. Which former Manchester United manager said: "Yes, Woodcock would have scored but his shot was too perfect"?

29. **Name the radio commentator who said: "Ian Rush. Deadly ten times out of ten. But that wasn't one of them."**

30. Who is the TV commentator who said: "Oh, he had an eternity to play that ball......but he took too long over it"?

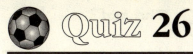

31. Which former Manchester City and Everton defender once said: "I can't promise anything but I can promise 100 per cent"?

32. Name the TV commentator who said: "McCarthy shakes his head in agreement with the referee."

33. Who said of his side's 4-3 win over Leicester: "Games like this are probably why Kevin Keegan went grey and Terry McDermott's hair is white"?

34. Which Dutch striker said of an extra £7,000 a week offered to him as: "Good enough for the homeless but not an international striker"?

35. Which former World Footballer of the Year said of being a substitute: "At the moment I feel like a Ferrari being driven by a traffic warden"?

36. Which Premiership defender said of coming to England: "It won't be easy here, and any normal, intelligent person would have stayed at Inter"?

37. Which player said after being sent-off for foul and abusive language: "Industrial language is part and parcel of the game. If I had been sent off every time I have sworn at an official I'd only have completed 100 games in my career"?

38. Which international striker said of coming to England: "I did not come here on holiday or to enjoy myself. I came here to play and become a legend in London with Chelsea"?

39. Which manager said of Florin Raducioiu: "He went missing on the way to the Stockport game because he thought he was going to be sub. He had every chance of playing that night, but he was shopping with his in-laws in Harvey Nichols"?

40. Which manager of Exeter said of his side's chances of beating Aston Villa in the FA Cup: "I've seen Desert Orchid fall. I've seen Bestie refuse a drink. I've seen Emlyn Hughes buy one. So you never know"?

41. **Which former England international said: "Playing is like a bug with me. I don't know when I'll be cured. I still get the same buzz. It's a magnificent life, being a professional footballer, and I'm frightened of going too soon"?**

42. Name the former Newcastle manager who said: "Sir John Hall was a multi-millionaire when I came back to Newcastle. With all the players I've bought, I'm trying to make him just an ordinary millionaire."

43. **Which former Tottenham manager once said: "I always tell young managers to pick their best team at the start of the season, write it on a piece of paper and tuck it away in a drawer. Half way through the season, if things are going wrong, look at those names again......because the first team you pick each season is always you best team"?**

44. Who said after Manchester United were knocked out of the European Cup by Galatasaray: "I just sat at home watching TV - and it wasn't even switched on"?

45. **Which radio commentator said: "Ray Wilkins sends an inch-perfect pass to no-one in particular"?**

46. Which manager once said: "Who's want to be a football manager? People like me who are too old to be a player, too poor to be a director and too much in love with the game to be an agent"?

47. **Which goalkeeper said: "One of the old trainers, John Latimer, said to me: 'Goalkeepers have got to be crackers and daft. You, son, have got the qualities of an international.' I took it as a compliment"?**

48. Who said of living with a footballer: "I've been married for 17 years and been to 14 clubs, lived in six houses, five hotels and seven rented places. As for John, he is so wrapped up in his job, I've even heard him giving Gerald Sinstadt a TV interview.....in his sleep"?

49. **Which manager said: "I know we are the team everyone loves to hate. They blame us for everything, from England's failure in the World Cup to the rising price in plums"?**

50. Which former Premiership striker said: "A goalscorer is paid to get hurt inside the 18-yard box and to die inside the 6-yard box"?

51. **Who said after suffering a horrific injury in a challenge with Wimbledon's John Fashanu: "John Fashanu was playing professional football without due care and attention"?**

52. Which former manager said of Kevin Keegan: "It was great for the game that Keegan came back to Newcastle. For a long period the club had been not through thick and thin, but through thin and thinner"?

53. **Who said of a Tony Yeboah goal: "It was in the net in the time it takes a snowflake to melt on a hot stove"?**

54. Who said of Eric Cantona: "He is so mild-mannered when the volcano inside him isn't erupting"?

55. **Which former Luton manager said of their 3-2 win at Wolves: "I told my players that Alex Ferguson was here, that they could do themselves a bit of good. He was actually here to watch his lad Darren playing for Wolves, but my lot wouldn't know that, would they?"?**

56. Which former World Cup winning manager said: "The art of picking a national team is not necessarily to choose the best 11 players in the country, but the 11 who fit together best"?

57. **Who said of John fashanu: "I think John Fashanu is worth £30 million really. I only said £12 million because it's nearly Christmas"?**

58. Which Premiership striker said after leaving Cambridge United: "I knew I couldn't take any more when, one day in training, a player shouted 'feet' meaning that's where he wanted the ball - and he was punished by being made to do 40 press-ups"?

59. **Who said of Paul Gascoigne leaving for Lazio: "I am pleased for him but it's like watching your mother-in-law drive off the cliff in your new car"?**

60. Which Scottish player said on the eve of their vital European Championship tie in Switzerland: "Our attitude is exactly right. Every player in the squad would give his left arm to play in this game. Well, maybe not the goalkeepers"?

61. **Which TV pundit said: "Trevor Steven might have scored there if he'd chanced his arm with his left foot"?**

62. Who said on the eve of the 1992 European Championship: "I expect to win. Let me do the worrying - that's what I'm paid for. You get your feet up in front of the telly, get a few beers in and have a good time"?

63. **Which radio commentator said of the 3,231 fans at a Wimbledon-Luton match: "The spectators showed the stewards to their seats"?**

64. Which former Sheffield United manager said: "They've been loyal to me. When I came here, they said there would be no money, and they've kept their word"?

65. **Which veteran striker said: "It's best being a striker. If you miss five, then score the winner, you're a hero. The goalkeeper can play a blinder, then let one in.....and he's a villain"?**

66. Who replied when asked what an American was doing playing in goal for Millwall: "Trying to keep the ball out"?

67. **Which former Blackburn manager said: "If we score more goals than they do, we will win"?**

68. Who said on his first game as Newcastle manager: "You just sit there, pretend you know what you are doing, and hope you get it right"?

69. **Which legendary England winger said: "I played in the First Division until I was 50. That was a mistake. I could have gone on for another two years"?**

70. Which former Scotland manager said: "To me, pressure is being homeless or unemployed, not trying to win a football match"?

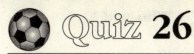

71. **Name the veteran manager who said on his return to management at Bristol Rovers: "It's hard to believe that so many professional in this country haven't been taught how to kick a football correctly."**

72. Which club owner said of Vinnie Jones' video that showed violence and cheating: "He must be a mosquito brain to say what he's said"?

73. **Which former Premiership manager said in 1990: "Ten years from now, Paul Gascoigne might have proved himself the biggest name in football, or he might have blown it. Either way, I will not be surprised"?**

74. Who said of Graeme Souness' decision to leave Rangers to manager Liverpool: "I believe he is making the biggest mistake of his life. Time will tell"?

75. **Who said on being awarded the OBE in June 1990: "My wife says it stands for 'Old Big'Ead"?**

76. "Now the players applaud the crowd at the end of a match. When I was playing, it was the other way round"?

77. **Which legendary manager said of playing youngsters: "If you don't put them in, you'll never know what you've got"?**

78. Which former Liverpool striker said: "When my playing career is over, I'll return to Liverpool and stand on the Kop just like I used to when I was a kid"?

79. **Which former QPR manager said: "I am not difficult to get on with. I am just difficult to get to know"?**

80. Which former England striker said: "There is no point in looking back in life. I had a marvelous time playing football, travelled the world, played with and against some great players. But I got old. People ask me why I gave up football. I tell them I didn't. Football gave me up"?

81. **Name the former Argentinean manager who said: "The player who kicks the last penalty either has the key to the hotel or the plane tickets home"?**

82. Which England veteran said in October 1989: "Every year I play now is an extra. The longer it's gone on, the more I've enjoyed it"?

83. **Which former Wolves manager remarked: "People say Steve Bull's first touch isn't good, but he usually scores with his second"?**

84. When he was in charge of Derby, who said: "A mistake is only a mistake when it is done twice"?

85. **Which legendary player said of his first experience of watching England: "My father took me, as a very young boy, to see the great England, and I went to the match expecting so much. That was the day they lost 1-0 to the U.S.A. in the World Cup"?**

86. Which international goalkeeper said: "From watching Gordon Banks, I learnt about positioning. From watching Peter Bonetti, I learnt about agility. And from watching Lev Yashin, the great Russian goalkeeper dressed in all black, I learnt about projecting an invincible image"?

87. **Who said on life in Italy: "The most incredible thing was the way the Juventus players took their minds off a match. Ninety minutes before kick-off, some smoked cigarettes or drank a glass of wine. Everyone seemed to find that normal - except me"?**

88. Who gave this advice to Kenny Dalglish when he signed for Liverpool: "Don't over-eat and don't lose your accent"?

89. **Which England midfielder said after signing a seven-year contract in November 19??: "I never seriously thought about going abroad. Knowing I can play out my career with Spurs is brilliant"?**

90. Which England international said: "I got eight O-levels at school.....zero in every subject"?

91. **Which Premiership manager told his team: "If you have the ball, you command the game. If you kick and rush, it depends on luck"?**

92. Which former England coach said: "There is nothing you can know about football that cannot be learned from watching Germany. Physically, tactically, technically, mentally, they get it right almost every time"?

93. **Which former legendary manager said once: "I'm only surprised that people are surprised by surprise results in football"?**

94. Which Premiership manager said: "You have to remember, a goalkeeper is a goalkeeper because he can't play football"?

95. **Which international manager said of allowing players' wives and girlfriends into the team camp: "I've nothing against it. Love is good for footballers, as long as it is not at half-time"?**

96. Which Premiership manager had this message on his answerphone: "I'm sorry I'm not here at the moment. If you are the president of AC Milan, Barcelona or Real Madrid, I'll get back to you"?

97. **Which former manager said: "Southampton is a very well-run outfit from Monday to Friday. It's Saturday we've got a problem with"?**

98. Who said after his side drew with Newcastle in May 1996: "Me feel sorry for Kevin Keegan? When he's got Asprilla and Barton and Clark on the bench?"?

99. **Which England captain said after England's 1-1 draw in a friendly against Portugal: "At least we got a point"?**

100. Which Premiership manager said of his trade: "Management is a seven-days-a-week job. The intensity of it takes it's toll on your health. Some people want to go on for ever, and I obviously don't. I saw Alan Hansen playing golf three times a week, and it got me thinking"?

101. **Which manager left this message on his answerphone after being sacked by Birmingham: "Kristine (his wife) has gone shopping and I'm at the job centre, looking for employment. Funny old game, isn't it?"?**

102. Which radio commentator said: "Barmby stood out like a Pamela Anderson in a sea of Claire Raynors"?

103. **Which fromer England manager said: "This is a great job - until a ball is kicked"?**

104. Which legendary manager once said: "The secret of being a manager is to keep the six players who hate you away from the five who are undecided"?

105. **Which England goalscorer said in 1970: "It's easy to beat Brazil. You just stop them getting twenty yards from your goal"?**

106. Which former European Footballer of the Year said: "In my life I have had two big vices: smoking and playing football. Football has given me everything, but smoking nearly took it all away"?

107. **Which famous Brazilian said of the difference between South American and European football: "Our football comes from the heart, theirs comes from the mind"?**

108. Which former Manchester United player once said: "I could join Alcoholics Anonymous. Only problem is I can't remain anonymous"?

109. **Which Italian defender said of his treatment of Maradona during a match: "It is not dancing school"?**

110. Which famous Hungarian stated: "I am grateful to my father for all the coaching he did not give me"?

111. **Which former England manager said: "All managers are frustrated players"?**

112. Which former Newcastle and England star said of his club: "I have heard of players selling dummies. But this club keeps buying them"?

113. **Which Brazilian remarked in 1982: "Football became popular because it was an art. But now too many pitches are becoming battlefields"?**

114. Which former manager said: "I'm as bad a judge as Walter Winterbottom - he gave me only two caps"?

115. **Which Irish player remarked after he swapped shirts with Ruud Gullit in the 1988 European Championship: "When he gets mine home, he'll wonder who the bloody hell's it is"?**

116. Who said of Italian club Pisa's bid for his son: "They couldn't afford him even if they threw in the leaning tower"?

117. **Which WBA player said of seeing the Great Wall of China: "When you've seen one wall, you've seen the lot"?**

118. Which former Aberdeen manager said of signing Charlie Nicholas in 1988: "He has two arms and legs, same as the rest of our players, but once he finds his feet I'm convinced he'll do well"?

119. **Who said after scoring for Liverpool in 1988: "As the ball came over I remembered what Graham Taylor said about my having no right foot - so I headed it in"?**

120. Who once said of Paul Gascoigne: "he is accused of being arrogant, unable to cope with the press and a boozer. Sounds like he's got a chance to me"?

121. **Which television pundit said of Italian Marco Tardelli: "He's been responsible for more scar-tissue than the surgeons of Harefield hospital"?**

122. Which charismatic manager said in 1983: "It's bloody tough being a legend"?

123. **Which manager said: "One of the main reasons why I never became England manager was because the Football Association thought that I would take over and run the show. They were dead right"?**

124. Juventus owner, Gianni Agnelli, described which England player as being "a soldier of war with the face of a child"?

125. **Which former England captain said of his drinking days: "Even after a skinful, I don't have a hangover and can still be up with the others"?**

126. Which manager said in the 1990 World Cup: "We'll start worrying about the Italians when we sober up tomorrow"?

127. **Which television summariser said in the 1990 World Cup: "I've just seen Gary Lineker shake hands with Jurgen Klinsmann - it's a wonder Klinsmann hasn't fallen down"?**

128. About which Dutch player was it stated: "He knows the game from A to Z and if the alphabet had any more letters, he would know those as well"?

129. **Who said to his team before extra-time in a World Cup Final: "You've done it once, now win it again"?**

130. Which famous club chairman once said: "I know I'm difficult to deal with. It's because I'm not logical"?

131. Which former Aston Villa manager said: "I have told my players never to believe what I say about them in the papers"?

132. Which Scottish manager once remarked: "They serve a drink in Glasgow called the Souness - one half and you're off"?

133. Which manager in 1987 described Wimbledon as "the borstal of football"?

134. Which former England manager said in 1991: "A manager can never say always and can never say never"?

135. Who said when he become the first paid football director: "Only women and horses work for nothing"?

136. Which international manager said in Euro '96: "If I walked on water, my critics would say it was because I couldn't swim"?

137. Which international defender said on life in English football: "I came to this country to play football, not to be a kick-boxer, but there seems to be one in every side we play"?

138. Which England legend said of European football: "They know on the Continent that European football without the English is like a hot dog without mustard"?

139. Which legendary European footballer said: "The failure to understand the physical and mental strains on a professional is behind the widely held belief that footballers are stupid"?

140. Which manager said of the support on the eve of his team's game with England in Euro '96: "It's 2,000 of us against 70,000 drunkards"?

141. Which TV summariser previewed the Portugal-Czech Republic Euro '96 game by stating: "I'm looking forward to seeing some sexy football"?

142. Which former England goalscorer said: "Football is a simple game where 22 players play against each other and in the end Germany wins"?

143. Which England international said in 1971: "Soccer in England is a grey game, played on grey days by grey people"?

144. Which legendary footballer once said: "A penalty is a cowardly way to score a goal"?

145. Which Dutch international once said: "If I'd wanted to be an individual, I'd have taken up tennis"?

146. Which former England manager once stated: "Football is a simple game. The hard part is making it look simple"?

147. Who told Gareth Southgate after his penalty miss in Euro '96: "Why didn't you just belt it?"?

148. Which Scottish player said on the eve of Euro '96: "For the first match we'll be underdogs, and for the next two we'll be even bigger underdogs - even underpups"?

149. Which TV summariser said during the England-Spain game in Euro '96: "Three fresh men, three fresh legs"?

150. Which international manager said in 1983: "There's no rapport with referees these days. If you say anything you get booked, and if you don't they send you off for dumb insolence"?

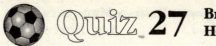

1. **Which manager won three FA Cups in the 1960s with Tottenham?**

2. Which manager won two successive FA Cups in the 1980s with Tottenham?

3. **Who was Southampton's manager when they lifted the FA Cup in 1976?**

4. Who was the coach for Coventry City's victory in the 1987 FA Cup?

5. **Which manager won the FA Cup with Manchester City in 1969?**

6. What was unusual about Preston North End's manager when they won the 1938 FA Cup?

7. **Who was West Ham's manager for their 1975 FA Cup victory?**

8. Who was West Bromwich Albion's manager for their last FA Cup victory in 1968?

9. **Which manager won two FA Cups, nine years apart, and with the same club, in the 1960s and 1970s?**

10. Who managed Nottingham Forest for their FA Cup win in 1959, when they beat Luton Town 2 - 1?

11. **Which manager took over at Hereford United in August 1995?**

12. Which two managers took control at Rotherham United in September 1994?

13. **At the start of the 1996/7 season, who was the longest serving manager in the first division, having taken over his club in March 1984?**

14. How many Division One teams had player-managers at the start of the 1996-7 season?

15. **Who was appointed Swansea City player-manager in February 1996?**

1. **Bill Nicholson** 2. Keith Burkinshaw 3. **Lawrie McMenemy** 4. John Sillett 5. **Joe Mercer** 6. There was no manager 7. **John Lyall** 8. Alan Ashman 9. **Bill Shankly** 10. Billy Walker 11. **Graham Turner** 12. Archie Gemmil and John McGovern 13. **John Rudge (Port Vale)** 14. 9 - Barnsley, Grimsby, Oldham, Portsmouth, QPR, Reading, Southend, Swindon, Tranmere 15. **Jan Molby**

16. Which Premiership club has, at the start of the 1996-97 season, had the most manager changes since the Second World War?

17. **Which Nationwide side has, at the beginning of the 1996/7 season, had the most managers since World War Two?**

18. Which 1996/7 Premiership manager has on his answerphone: "I'm sorry I'm not here at the moment. If you are the president of AC Milan, Barcelona or Real Madrid, I'll get back to you"?

19. **Which Premiership manager has his birthday on New Year's Eve?**

20. Who was the 1995/6 Division One Manager of the Year?

21. **With which team did Tony Pullis receive his Division Three Manager of the Year award at the end of the 1995-96 season?**

22. Which manager led Plymouth to a promotion in 1996, making it four promotions in seven years, following two with Notts County and one with Huddersfield?

23. **Bolton Wanderers manager Charles Foweraker was the first to do what?**

24. Which manager took his team to both of the two Rumbelows Cup finals?

25. **Which manager saw his team win the 1995-96 Scottish Coca Cola Cup?**

26. Who was the losing manager in the 1995/6 Scottish FA Cup final?

27. **For which club was Paul Fairclough the Vauxall Conference Manager of the Year, in 1995/6?**

28. Which former Premiership manager was sacked after ten matches as the coach of Mexican club Guadalajara?

29. **Who became the shortest serving manager in League history, surviving only three days at Scunthorpe in 1959?**

30. Who, in 1984, was named as manager at Crystal Palace, but changed his mind four days later, without signing a contract?

16. Coventry City - 20 17. **Darlington - 25** 18. Joe Kinnear 19. **Alex Ferguson** 20. Peter Reid 21. **Gillingham** 22. Neil Warnock 23. **Win the FA Cup** 24. Alex Ferguson 25. **Roy Aitken (Aberdeen)** 26. Jim Jefferies (Hearts) 27. **Stevenage Borough** 28. Ossie Ardiles 29. **Bill Lambton** 30. Dave Bassett

31. **Which League club has had the fewest number of managers, by the end of the 1996-97 season?**

32. Who was the first man to achieve the Championship/FA Cup double as player-manager?

33. **Who was England's longest serving manager?**

34. Which manager won the 1958 and 1959 League championships with Wolves?

35. **Who was the first manager to achieve the League and Cup double at Arsenal?**

36. How many matches was John Toshack manager of Wales?

37. **Who was the first player-manager, in the old First Division, when he played for QPR, 1968-9?**

38. Who is the only manager to win the League Championship with Ipswich Town?

39. **For how long was Brian Clough manager of Leeds United in 1974?**

40. Who was the first manager to win the FA Cup with two different sides?

41. **Name the three managers that have won League Championships with two different clubs.**

42. Who was Coventry City's player-manager in 1990-91?

43. **Who is the longest serving manager in Scottish League football, spending 17 years in charge?**

44. How many trophies did Bob Paisley win with Liverpool?

45. **Which manager coached both Watford and Sheffield United in the 1987-8 season?**

46. With what club did Aston Villa manager Brian Little spend only 49 days in charge?

47. **Which 1996/7 manager has scored the fastest ever first class goal at Wembley?**

48. Who was the last Second Division manager to win the FA Cup?

49. **Which two 1995-96 Premiership managers have been sent off for England in full internationals?**

50. Which British manager took over the Kuwait national side in 1986, and later went on to manage Vitoria Setubal in Portugal?

51. **Which British manager coached at Athletico Bilbao in 1987?**

52. Which English manager was sacked from his foreign club in September 1987?

53. **Which British manager was sacked after only 94 days at Athletico Madrid?**

54. Which British manager had spells at Celta Vigo and Athletico Madrid?

55. **Who moved from Real Madrid to manage Real Sociedad in 1989?**

56. Who moved from Tottenham to take over at Espanol for only 41 days?

57. **Which British manager has coached four different teams, in three different countries since 1992?**

58. Who went from being the Czech national manager to Aston Villa in 1990?

59. **Who left Swedish team Malmo to become coach at Southend in August 1992?**

60. Which foreign manager joined the Premiership after leaving WBA in 1992?

61. Which ex-Chelsea manager moved to Kuwait to head Al-Arabi Sporting Club?

62. Who, in 1995, signed a contract to manage Norwegian club FC Start?

63. Which 1996-97 Premiership manager has led clubs in France and Japan?

64. Which Premiership manager has coached in Turkey?

65. Which Englishman managed a country in the 1994 World Cup and helped them qualify for Euro 96?

66. Which European manager snubbed Blackburn Rovers in 1997?

67. Who became Celtic's manager in 1993, twenty years after leaving as a player?

68. Who resigned as Coventry manager in October 1993, ten minutes after 5-1 defeat by QPR?

69. Which Brit became Zambian manager, two months after the side lost 18 players in an air crash?

70. Which St. Mirren manager resigned to persue a coaching career in Florida?

71. Which Brit became coach of Spanish club Seville in May 1986?

72. Who left Sampdoria to become player-manager at Glasgow Rangers?

73. Who has managed clubs which include Middlesborough, Millwall, Bolton and Arsenal in recent years?

74. Who made his move into management by becoming player-manager at Sheffield Wednesday?

75. Which two men became joint player-coaches at Charlton, in July 1991?

76. Which manager was released as a player by Monaco, following an ankle injury, in April 1991?

77. **Who managed Italy to their 1982 World Cup win?**

78. Who was the Argentinian manager when they lifted the World Cup in 1986?

79. **Who are the only two men to have won the World Cup as both players and managers?**

80. In the 1994 World Cup, who was the manager of the only team to have played in all of the World Cup finals?

81. **Who were the two managers in charge for Holland's 1994 World Cup campaign?**

82. Who was the Spanish manager during the 1994 World Cup?

83. **Who went from managing Millwall to the Republic of Ireland?**

84. Who took England to four successive World Cup finals?

85. **Who was the manager of AC Milan when they lifted the World Club Championship in 1994?**

86. Who was in charge when England failed to reach the 1978 World Cup final?

87. **Who was England's manager for the 1982 World Cup?**

88. Who took England to a quarter-final and a semi-final in two successive World Cups?

89. **Who was manager when England finished third in the European Championships?**

90. How many England managers have represented their country at senior level football?

76. Glenn Hoddle 77. **Enzo Bearzot** 78. Carlos Bilardo 79. **Mario Zagalo (Brazil) and Franz Beckenbauer (Germany)** 80. Carlos Alberto Parreira 81. **Dick Advocaat (qualifiers) and Johan Cruyff (finals)** 82. Javier Clemente 83. **Mick McCarthy** 84. Walter Winterbottom 85. **Fabio Capello** 86. Don Revie 87. **Ron Greenwood** 88. Bobby Robson 89. **Sir Alf Ramsey (1948)** 90. 6 - Ramsey, Mercer, Revie, Robson, Venables, Hoddle

91. Who was in charge of England when the World Cup was held in Chile?

92. Who have been the last three Scottish managers?

93. Who was Northern Ireland's manager for 13 years, from 1980-93?

94. Who took over from Roy Hodgson as manager of Switzerland for Euro 96?

95. Who was the French coach for Euro 96?

96. Which manager won Euro 96?

97. Who was the Italian manager that was sacked after Italy's poor results in Euro 96?

98. Who led Holland in Euro 96?

99. Which manager won the League Cup three years in a row in the Eighties?

100. Who was West Ham's manager when they won the 1965 Cup Winners Cup?

101. Which two managers have led English sides to two consecutive European Cups?

102. Who was the manager of the 1995 European Cup champions?

103. Which acting manager lost out in the 1995 Cup Winners' Cup final?

104. Who was manager for Everton's 1985 Cup Winners' Cup victory?

105. Who is the last manager to have won the European Cup with a British side?

106. Who was in charge for a British club's last victory in the Cup Winners' Cup?

107. Who was the manager when a British club last lited the UEFA Cup?

108. Who was the manager of the last Scottish team to win a European trophy?

109. Which manager led Chelsea to an FA Cup victory in 1970 and a Cup Winners Cup victory in 1971?

110. Who was the manager of the British team that beat Inter Milan in the 1994/5 UEFA Cup?

111. Who was the manager to lead his British club to win the last Fairs Cup, before it became the UEFA Cup?

112. Who was the losing FA Cup final manager in 1994?

113. Who managed the FA Cup final team that lost to Tottenham in 1982?

114. Which manager won the 1995 FA Cup?

115. who was the losing manager in the 1995 Coca Cola Cup final?

116. Which manager lost in the final of both the FA Cup and League Cup finals in 1993?

117. Who was the manager of the Scottish league champions in the 1994/5 season?

118. Who is the only manager to have led Raith Rovers to a Scottish League Cup success, when they beat Celtic in 1995?

119. Who was the manager of Celtic when they won the Scottish FA Cup?

120. Which manager wnet from Birmingham City to own Peterborough United?

121. **Which former Everton player was managing third division Chester City at the start of the 1995/6 season?**

122. Which former England international was in charge at the beginning of the 1995/6 season?

123. **Who moved from Aston Villa to Wolves to Watford, with a pwriod as a national coach in between?**

124. Which ex-england internatioal took over at Portsmouth in February 1995?

125. **Who took Wycombe Wanderers from non-league football to the Second division for the start of the 1994/5 season?**

126. Who was manager of Oldham Athletic from July 1982 until November 1994?

127. **Who went from the Scottish Premier league to manage Brighton and Hove Albion in 1993?**

128. Who took over as player-manager at Plymouth Argile in March 1992?

129. **Which player-manager won the 1994/5 First division title?**

130. Which manager moved to Leicester and then Wolves after being player-manager at Reading?

131. **Who went from being a player-manager at Barnsley to assistant coach at Premiership Middlesborough?**

132. Which manager rejoined Norwich for his second spell, following an unsuccessful time at Everton?

133. **Who brought Nottingham Forest back into the top division, and then returned to manage Manchester City?**

134. Which former Portsmouth boss took Derby County into the Premiership?

135. **Who did Bryan Robson succeed as Middlesborough manager?**

---

121. **Kevin Ratcliffe** 122. Ray Clemence 123. **Graham Taylor** 124. Terry Fenwick 125. **Martin O'Neill** 126. Joe Royle 127. **Liam Brady** 128. Peter Shilton 129. **Bryan Robson** 130. Mark McGhee 131. **Viv Anderson** 132. Mike Walker 133. **Frank Clark** 134. Jim Smith 135. **Lennie Lawrence**

136. Which FA Cup winning manager took over at Ipswich fron Mick McGiven?

137. **Which Premiership manager won the 1983 Player of the Year award?**

138. Who was the last Scottish manager to beat England in an international?

139. **Which former Liverpool player was Oxford manager when they were relegated in 1988?**

140. Which former international manager was also in charge at Everton?

141. **Which club sacked manager Don O'Riordan the day after his side were beaten 8-1 by Scunthorpe in October 1995?**

142. Which former England captain managed Arsenal btween 1962 and 1966?

143. **Which England legend managed Bolton Wanderers between 1968 and 1970?**

144. Which European Cup winning manager was in charge at Brighton and Hove Albion from 1973 to 1974?

145. **Who managed Bristol Rovers before moving to QPR?**

146. Who was the manager of Fulham in 1968, before moving to coach abroad?

147. **Who was the manager of Leeds United that went on to manage Scotland?**

148. Who was the Leeds United manager before Howard Wilkinson?

149. **What club did Jack Charlton manage before becoming the Republic of Ireland manager?**

150. Who managed Sheffield Wednesday from 1983 to 1988?

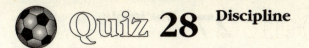

1. **What is the highest number of sendings off to occur in a season (1994-95) in all competitions from clubs in the Premier League and the Nationwide divisions?**

   A. 365, B. 376, C.367

2. Which League club had the worst record for sendings off in the 1995-96 season with 10?

   A. Hartlepool, B. Wimbledon, C. Norwich City

3. **Which three League clubs did not have a player sent off in first team football in the 1995-96 season?**

4. How many players were shown the red card on November 20 1982, to set a record for the number of sendings off in a day in League football?

   A. 10, B. 8, C. 15

5. **What is the lowest number of League dismissals in a season since the Second World War?**

   A. 3, B. 12, C. 10

6. Against which team was Alan Mullary the first ever Englishman to be sent off in a full international?

   A. Norway, B. Scotland, C. Yugoslavia

7. **Who was sent off for England in a World Cup qualifier against Poland?**

   A. Malcolm McDonald, B. Graham Roberts, C. Alan Ball

8. Who was the third player ever to be sent off in a full England international?

   A. Ray Wilkins, B. Trevor Cherry, C. Terry Butcher

9. **What was Ray Wilkins shown the red card for when he became the only Englishman to be sent off in the World Cup Finals?**

   A. Dissent, B. Throwing the ball at the referee, C. Professional foul

10. Against which team was Robbie Fowler sent off in an England Under 21 international?

    A. Wales, B. Austria, C. Germany

Quiz 27 — Discipline

11. **Against which country was Kevin Keegan sent off in an England Under 23 international in 1972?**

    A. West Germany, B. East Germany, C. Romania

12. Who was shown the red card in an England Under 21 match against Scotland in 1982?

    A. Bryan Robson, B. Peter Beardsley, C. Mark Hateley

13. **Who is the only person to be sent off in an England B match, in 1990?**

    A. Neil Webb, B. Paul Gascoigne, C. Steve Bull

14. Who were the teams involved when five players were sent off in the 1996-97 season?

    A. Chesterfield and Gillingham, B. Plymouth and Watford, C. Chesterfield and Plymouth

15. **Which League team were the first to have four players sent off in one game, and still managed a 1-1 draw, in 1992?**

    A. Wigan, B. Hereford United, C. Scarborough

16. How many people were sent off in the 1994 Anglo-Italian Cup match between Sheffield United and Udinese?

    A. 6, B. 2, C. 4

17. **How many players were sent off in the 1993 South American Super Cup quater final between Gremio from Brazil and Penarol from Uruguay?**

    A. 9, B. 7, C. 8

18. Who was shown the red card five times in the 1987-88 season?

    A. Vinnie Jones, B. Dave Caldwell, C. Terry Hurlock

19. **What is the world record for the quickest sending off, held by Giuseppe Lorenzo in an Italian League match in 1990?**

    A. ten seconds, B. five seconds, C. eight seconds

20. Who holds the record for the fastest Premier League sending off at just 72 seconds?

    A. Vinnie Jones, B. Tim Flowers, C. Roy Keane

11. East Germany 12. Mark Hateley **13. Neil Webb** 14. Chesterfield and Plymouth **15. Hereford United** 16. 5 (4 players and United manager Dave Bassett) **17.** 8 18. Dave Caldwell **19. 10 seconds 20.** Tim Flowers

21. **Jose Batista holds the record for the fastest World Cup sending off at 55 seconds in the 1986 tournament. Which country was he playing for?**

    A. Spain, B. Argentina, C. Uruguay

22. Which Scotsman holds the record for the most sendings off in a career?

    A. Willie Johnston, B. Graeme Souness, C. Billy Bremner

23. **Who is the only player to have been sent off in an FA Cup final?**

    A. Andrei Kanchelskis, B. Paul Gascoigne, C. Kevin Moran

24. Who was sent off in the 1994 League Cup final?

    A. Roy Keane, B. Dalian Atkinson, C. Andrei Kanchelskis

25. **Which two players were sent off in the 1974 Charity Shield?**

    A. Tommy Smith and Norman Hunter, B. Johnny Giles and John Toshack, C. Billy Bremner and Kevin Keegan

26. Which country were the last to have somebody sent off at Wembley?

    A. Japan, B. England, C. Holland

27. **Which two players had their dismissals revoked in the 1995-6 season?**

    A. Vinnie Jones and Mick Harford, B. Henning Berg and Roy Keane, C. Vinnie Jones and Henning Berg

28. Which club holds the record for the most bookings for a single League team in one game, at 10?

    A. Wimbledon, B. Mansfield Town, C. Exeter City

29. **Team mates Mick Flanagan and Derek Hales were sent off for fighting each other at which club in 1979?**

    A.Colchester United, B. Charlton, C. Derby County

30. Who was suspended for nine matches and fined a then record #3,000 for breaking Glenn Cockerill's jaw?

    A. Paul Davis, B. Steve Davis, C. Pat Jennings.

Quiz 28 — Discipline

31. **Who was suspended for nine matches and fined £600 for a clash of heads with a referee whilst on loan with WBA in 1992?**

    A. Graham Roberts, B. Micky Droy, C. Frank Sinclair.

32. Who was originally banned for 12 matches in 1995 for violent conduct against Raith, and later jailed for three months for assault?

    A.Duncan Ferguson, B. Mark Hateley, C. Joe Jordan.

33. **Which manager was banned from the touchline for the rest of the season after striking spectators at a League Cup match in 1989?**

    A.Alex Ferguson, B. Brian Clough, C. Graham Souness.

34. Who was fined 8,500 following a newspaper criticism of his former club in 1989?

    A.Cive Allen, B. Ian Bright, C. Paul McGrath.

35. **Which two clubs were fined 50,000 pounds each and deducted points following a mass player brawl in 1990?**

    A.Liverpool and Manchester United, B. Leeds and Manchester United, C. Arsenal and Manchester United.

36. Which player received a three match ban for 'feigning injury' in 1992, later cancelled?

    A.Paul Gascoigne, B. Gordon Durie, C. David Hopkin.

37. **Who was fined 1,000 pounds for spitting at Leeds fans in 1993?**

    A. Roy Keane, B. Julian Dicks, C. Eric Cantona.

38. What was Tottenham's original punishment for their financial irregularities in 1994?

    A. £600,000 fine and 12 Premiership points deducted, B. £150,000 fine and 12 points deducted. C. £300,000 fine and 6 points deducted.

39. **Who was fined for dropping his shorts at spectators?**

    A. Robbie Fowler, B. Dennis Wise, C. Arthur Fowler.

40. Who was fined for swearing at Kevin Keegan after a match in 1995?

    A. Alex Ferguson, B.Vinnie Jones, C. David Ginola.

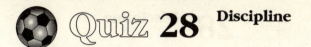

41. Who was the first person to reach 61 disciplinary points in a season?

A. Trevor Brooking, B. Terry Hurlock, C. Ron Harris.

42. Who were suspended for 2 games by UEFA for brawling in a European game?

A. Ian Wright(Arsenal) and Jari Litmanen (Ajax). B. Jari Litmanen and Vanio Shishkov (CSKA Sofia), C. David Batty and Graeme Le Saux (Blackburn).

43. Faustino Asprilla was found guilty of an elbowing/headbutting incident with which player?

A. Nigel Winterburn, B. Keith Curle, C. Phil Babb.

44. Who was Sunderland's club captain that was banned for their 1985 Milk Cup final?

A.Peter Reid, B. Shaun Elliot, C. Tony Coton.

45. Which former West Ham player had his sending off revoked in the 1994-95 season?

A. Alvin Martin, B. Julian Dicks, C. Ian Dowie.

46. Who has the time of five seconds for the second fastest booking, behind Vinnie Jones's record of 3 seconds?

A.Gary Lineker, B. Vinnie Jones, C. Tony Adams.

47. Which two teams were involved in the 1991 Scottish Cup quarter-final when four players were shown the red card?

A. Raith-Rangers, B. Rangers-Celtic, C. Celtic-Hearts.

48. The sending off of how many players from one team resulted in the abandonment of a Brazilian Cup match in 1993?

A. 3, B.2, C.5.

49. Which team had three players sent off in a Second Division League game against Derby in April 1992?

A.Newcastle, B.Brentford, C.Southend.

50. Which goalkeeper holds the record for the fastest dismissal in English domestic football?

A.Dave Beasant, B.Mark Smith, C.-Mike Walker.

51. **Sergei Dirkach holds the record for the fastest European game sending off. For which club was he dismissed, after 90 seconds, in 1991?**

   A.Galatasaray, B.Dynamo Moscow, C. Barcelona.

52. Which Premiership club had the most sendings off in the 1995-96 season, all in the League?

   A.QPR, B. Wimbledon, C. Leeds.

53. **How many sendings off were there in the Premiership in the 1995-96 season?**

   A. 57, B. 36, C. 82.

54. How many sendings off were there in the play-off games in the 1995-96 season?

   A.9, B. 12, C.1.

55. **Who was the last person to be sent off for Northern Ireland?**

   A. Iain Dowie, B.Norman Whiteside, C. Mick McCarthy.

56. Who was shown the red card for Scotland against Japan in 1995?

   A.Craig Burley, B. Gordon Durie, C. John Spencer.

57. **Who was sent off for the Republic of Ireland in their game against Mexico in 1996?**

   A.Paul McGrath, B. Liam Daish, C.Andy Townsend.

58. Julian Dicks and Jason Dodd were both sent off against which country in different games for the England Under 21s?

   A. USA, B. Mexico, C. West Germany.

59. **Who was the first player to be sent off for England at any level?**

   A. Dixie Dean, B.Stan Anderson, C. Samuel Weaver.

60. Who was sent off for England in an Under 21 game in May 1996?

   A.Terry Cooke, B. Chris Waddle, C. Kevin Beattie.

---

61. Which country was Gilbert Dresch representing when he was sent off at Wembley against England in a 1977 World Cup qualifier?

A. Belgium, B.Luxembourg, C. France.

62. Four clubs saw their club captains suspended for their League Cup finals in which four consecutive years?

A. 1896-1899, B. 1982-1985, C. 1970-1973.

63. Which team had two players dismissed in a play-off final at Wembley in 1994?

A. Crystal Palace, B. Stockport, C. Carlisle.

64. Who was only the second person to be sent off in the FA Cup at Wembley?

A. Lee Dixon, B. Steve Foster, C. Frank Sinclair.

65. Which former QPR player was booked 64 times in ten seasons and answered two disrepute charges concerning newspaper articles?

A. Les Ferdinand, B. Stan Bowles, C. Mark Dennis.

66. Which team were fined in 1990 for failing play a League Cup game due to injuries?

A. Middlesbrough, B. Chesterfield, C. Torquay

67. In which year was the disciplinary points system introduced?

A. 1962-63, B.1972-73, C. 1954-55.

68. Which player was fined in 1994 for making 'gestures' at QPR fans?

A. Ian Wright, B. Steve Bull, C. Sol Campbell.

69. Which English teams were banned from European competition for a year (suspended for five years) in 1996?

A.Millwall and Chelsea, B.Tottenham and Wimbledon, C.Coventry and Millwall.

70. Which club sacked Roger Stanislaus after he bacame the first British-based player to be found positive for taking performance enhancing drugs and banned for a year?

A. Leyton Orient, B. Doncaster Rovers, C. Barnet.

71. **To which club did Manchester United have to pay 20,000 pounds for illegally approaching 17 year-old David Brown?**

    A. Liverpool, B. West Brom, C. Oldham.

72. Which club were fined by UEFA for the behaviour of their 'unofficial' fans at an away leg in 1995?

    A. Arsenal, B. Chelsea, C.Juventas.

73. **Who was fined by the FA for a newspaper criticism of Eric Cantona in 1994?**

    A.Jimmy Greaves, B.John Giles, C. John Fashanu.

74. Who is the only player to have been sent off at Wembley in a major tournament?

    A.Kevin Keegan, B. Antonio Rattin, C. Christo Stoichkov.

75. **In what year was Boris Stankovic the first player to ever be sent off at Wembley?**

    A. 1904, B. 1948, C. 1954.

76. Which club was fined after arriving late for their League game at Darlington in 1994?

    A.Brighton, B.Preston, C. Mansfield.

77. **Which club were fined for fielding a Liverpool player registered on loan after the deadline, in 1995?**

    A.Sunderland, B. Watford, C.Motherwell.

78. Which Premiership club's chairman was fined for remarks to a referee at Arsenal in 1995?

    A.Manchester United, B.Chelsea, C. Blackburn Rovers.

79. **Which two clubs were fined after breaking rules when signing players from Australia, in 1993?**

    A.Arsenal and Notts Forest, B.Wrexham and Leicester, C.Aston Villa and Notts County.

80. Which team was fined by UEFA for a coin throwing incident during a european game in 1993?

    A.Panathinaikos, B.Atletico Madrid, C. Cardiff.

1. **What were Arsenal first known as in 1886?**

2. When did they turn professional?

3. **What was their first ground?**

4. When did they move to Highbury?

5. **What is the club's record victory?**

6. And their record defeat?

7. **When were Aston Villa formed?**

8. Where did they first play?

9. **In their first game, against Aston Brook St Mary's, they played one half of soccer and the other rugby. True or false?**

10. When did Barnet play their first League game?

11. **What was the score?**

12. What were Barnsley first known as?

13. **Who has been their most capped international?**

14. What were Birmingham City first known as?

15. **Where did they first play?**

16. Birmingham City hold the record for the highest number of players used in a season. How many and which season?

17. When were Blackburn Rovers formed?

18. Where did they play their home games at first?

19. Who is their record goalscorer in League football?

20. How many did he get?

21. What were Blackpool first known as?

22. When did they move to Bloomfield Road?

23. Which player holds the record for appearances for the club?

24. What is the record transfer fee they have received - and for who?

25. What were Bolton Wanderers first called?

26. What is the club's nickname?

27. The club lost it's first League game 6-3 in 1888. To who?

28. Who holds the record for being the club's most capped player?

29. What is the record transfer fee Brentford have received - and for who?

30. What is the record transfer fee Brighton have paid out - and for who?

16. 46 - 1995-96 17. 1875 18. They didn't - all their games in 1875-76 were played away because they had nowhere to play 19. Simon Garner 20. 168 21. South Shore 22. 1899 23. Jimmy Armfield with 568 24. £750,000 from QPR for Trevor Sinclair 25. Christ Church FC 26. The Trotters 27. Derby County 28. Nat Lofthouse 29. £720,000 from Wimbledon for Dean Holdsworth 30. £500,000 to Manchester United for Andy Ritchie

31. How many grounds have Brentford played their homes games at?

32. When did they move to Griffin Park?

33. Bristol Rovers have had four other names. 'Black Arabs' was one of them - true or false?

34. What were Cambridge United first known as?

35. When did they change it?

36. Who has been their most capped player?

37. What is Cardiff City's nickname?

38. What is the record transfer fee they have paid out - and for who?

39. What were Carlisle United first known as?

40. What has been the record transfer they have receieved for a player - and who is the player in question?

41. How many different homes have Charlton Athletic had?

42. How many times have they made the Valley their home?

43. The club was formed in 1905 - but by who?

44. Who is Chelsea's record goalscorer in one season - and how many did he get?

45. Who holds the record for appearances for Chelsea?

31. **Six**. 32. 1904 33. **True**, in 1883 34. Abbey United 35. 1949 36. Tom Finney for Northern Ireland, with seven full caps 37. **The Blubirds** 38. £180,000 to San Jose Earthquakes for Godfrey Ingham in 1982 39. **Shaddongate United** 40. £275,000 from Vancouver Whitecaps for Peter Beardsley in 1981 41. **Ten** 42. Three 43. A group of 14 and 15-year olds 44. Jimmy Greaves - 41 in 1960-61 45. Ron Harris - 655 between 1962 and 1980

46. Whose ground did Chester City share between 1990 and 1992?

47. **What is Chesterfield's nickname?**

48. What were Coventry first known as?

49. **Who has been their most capped player?**

50. Coventry have never won an European trophy. True or false?

51. **What is the record number of players who have scored for Crewe in one game?**

52. Who has been Crystal Palace's youngest League debutant - and at what age?

53. **When did Derby move to the Baseball Ground?**

54. How many grounds did Everton have before moving to Goodison Park?

55. **What was their previous name?**

56. Everton were the first club to win the Second Division title, First Division title and the FA Cup in successive seasons. True and false?

57. **Who is their record League goalscorer - and with how many?**

58. The same player holds the record for the number of individual goals scored in one season - how many?

59. **What is Exeter's nickname?**

60. How many homes have Fulham had?

46. Macclesfield Town's Moss Rose ground 47. **The Spireites** 48. Singers FC 49. **Peter Ndlovu (Zimbabwe)** 50. False - they won the European Fairs Cup in 1971 51. **Eight - when they beat Hartlepool 8-0 in 1995** 52. Phil Hoadley - 16 53. 1895 54. Three 55. **St Domingo FC** 56. True - between 1931 and 1933 57. Dixie Dean - with 349 58. 60 in 1927-28 59. **The Grecians** 60. 12

61. **Huddersfield Town have never won the FA Cup. True or False?**

62. What remains the club's record defeat?

63. **Who holds the record for the most appearances for Ipswich?**

64. What remains Ipswich's record Cup victory?

65. **What were Leicester City first known as?**

66. How many different names have Leyton Orient had?

67. **Who founded Liverpool?**

68. When did they form?

69. **When Liverpool beat Stromsgodset 11-0 in the European Cup-Winners Cup in 1974, how many players found the net?**

70. Who holds the record for number of FA Cup goals scored for Liverpool?

71. **Whose record did he beat?**

72. Who is Liverpool's record goalscorer?

73. **What were Manchester City first known as?**

74. Where was their first home?

75. **What were Manchester United first known as?**

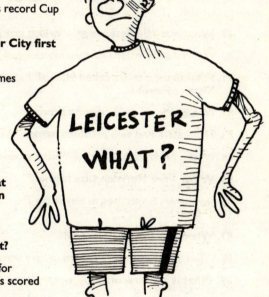

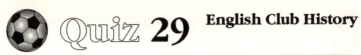
76. Manchester United have played at Old Trafford since 1910 - apart from eight years in the 1940's. Where did they go and why?

77. **Who holds the record for the number of League goals scored in one season for Manchester United?**

78. How many League goals did Bobby Charlton score for Manchester United?

79. **What was Middlesbrough previous ground called?**

80. Who holds the record for their most capped player?

81. **Millwall used to be called Millwall Rovers and Millwall Athletic. True or False?**

82. Who is their record League goalscorer?

83. **Newcastle had two previous names. What were they?**

84. What is Northampton's present home ground called?

85. **When were Norwich City formed?**

86. Nottingham Forest used to play at the Trent Bridge cricket ground. True or false?

87. **When was the club formed?**

88. When do Notts County claimed to have been formed?

89. **What is their record Cup victory?**

90. Who holds the record for the number of appearances for the club?

76. Maine Road - because of bomb damage to Old Trafford in World War Two 77. **Dennis Viollet - 32 in 1959-60** 78. 199 79. **Ayresome Park** 80. Wilf Mannion - with 26 for England 81. **True** 82. Teddy Sheringham 83. **Stanley and Newcastle East End** 84. Sixfields Stadium 85. **1902** 86. True - in 1880 87. **1865** 88. 1862 89. **15-0 over Rotherham Town in the 1885 FA Cup** 90. Alf Iremonger with

91. What competition did Notts County win in 1995?

92. What were Oldham first known as?

93. Who holds Portsmouth's record for the highes number of goals scored in one season?

94. When did Port Vale move to Vale Park?

95. Who is Preston's most capped player?

96. How many ground changes have QPR undertaken since being formed in 1885?

97. How many trophies did Sheffield Wednesday win in 1902-03?

98. Who holds the record for the most number of goals scored for Southampton?

99. When did they move to Dell?

100. What were Stockport County first known as?

101. What was Stoke City's first name?

102. Swansea's record Cup win was 12-0. But in what competition?

103. Who holds the record for the most appearances for Tottenham?

104. What was West Ham's first name?

105. When did Wimbledon reach Division One?

1. Who was the first player to score 200 goals in Scotland's Premier Division in December 1992?

2. Which player holds the individul scoring record in Scotland's Premier Division?

3. Who are the three players to have scored a hat-trick in a major final at Wembley?

4. Which player, in a first-class match, scored the fastest goal at Wembley?

5. Which player scored the second fastest goal at Wembley in a first-class match?

6. Which three players have scored a hat-trick in an FA Cup final?

7. Who was the first player to miss a penalty in a FA Cup final?

8. Who is the most recent player to have scored over 50 goals for a league club in one season?

9. Who was Second Division leading scorer for 1957-58, 1958-9 and 1959-60?

10. Which player scored five goals for England against Cyprus at Wembley on April 16 1975?

11. Who scored 13 goals in 38 appearances for Northern Ireland?

12. Who is the youngest player to have scored a hat-trick on his debut?

13. Which player has scored the most League hat-tricks in his career?

14. Which player has scored the most league hat-tricks in one season?

15. Which two teams have had the most individual scorers in one match?

1. **Ally McCoist** 2. Paul Sturrock (Dundee United) five goals against Morton. 3. **Stan Mortensen** (1953 FA Cup final), **Geoff Hurst** (1966 World Cup final) **David Speedie** (1985 Full Members Cup final). 4. Bryan Robson (England) 38 seconds v Yugoslavia in 1989. 5. **Bryan Robson (England) 44 seconds against Northern Ireland in 1982.** 6. Billy Townley (1890), Jimmy Logan (1894) and Stan Mortensen (1953) 7. **John Aldridge (Liverpool) v Wimbledon, 1988 FA Cup final.** 8. Steve Bull 52 goals for Wolves 1987/8 season 9. **Brian Clough** 10. Malcolm Macdonald 11. **Colin Clarke. 13 goals in 38 appearances.** 12. Alan Shearer aged 17 for Southampton v Arsenal April 9 1988. 13. 37 **by Dixie Dean (Everton and Tranmere)** 14. 9 by George Camsell (Middlesbrough) in Division Two 1926/7 15. Liverpool - nine against Stromsgodset in 1974. Stirling Albion - nine scorers against Selkirk in 1984

16. Which goalkeeper has scored most goals in a season?

17. **Who was the last player to score five goals in a top-flight match?**

18. When Oxford United beat Shrewsbury Town 6-0 on April 23 1996 in a Division Two match, what was unusual about all six goals?

19. **Who is England's top international goalscorer?**

20. Which player has scored the most goals in one League season?

21. **Who are the two joint top international goalscorers for Scotland?**

22. Who was the first player to score more than 30 goals in three successive seasons in top division football?

23. **Who is England's second highest international goalscorer?**

24. How many goals did Kevin Keegan score in his 63 games for England?

25. **Who has scored the most goals for Southampton?**

26. Which England player, between November 1991 and June 1982, scored seven goals in six consecutive international appearances?

27. **The Republic of Ireland beat Italy 1-0 in the 1994 World Cup who scored the winning goal?**

28. Newcastle United's Player of the Year for 1996 was also the club's top goalscorer. Who was he?

29. **How many goals did Paul Gascoigne score for Rangers in the 1995/6 season?**

30. Before moving to Arsenal how many goals did Ian Wright score for Crystal Palace in his 206 full appearances?

16. Arthur Birch 5 (all penalties) for Chesterfield Division Three North 1923/4 17. Andy Cole in Manchester United's 9-0 win over Ipswich, March 4 1995. 18. They were all headers. 19. Bobby Charlton (1958-70) 49 goals in 106 games. 20. Dixie Dean (Everton) 60 goals 1927/8. 21. Denis Law (1958-74) 30 goals in 55 games and Kenny Dalglish (1971-86) 30 goals in 102 games. 22. Alan Shearer 31 goals in 1993/4, 34 in 1994/5, 31 in 1995/6. 23. **Gary Lineker (1984-92) 48 goals in 80 games.** 24. 21 (1972-82) 25. **Mike Channon with 185** 26. Paul Mariner 27. **Ray Houghton.** 28. Les Ferdinand 29. 14 30. 90

31. Who was Euro 96's top goalscorer?

32. In the 1992 play-offs Blackburn Rovers secured promotion to the Premiership by beating Leicester. What was the score and who scored?

33. How many goals did Jimmy Greaves score for England?

34. In the 1994 Coca-Cola Cup final Aston Villa beat Manchester United 3-1, who scored Villa's three goals?

35. Aberdeen beat Dundee 2-0 in the 1996 Scottish Coca-Cola Cup final, who scored the goals?

36. Which player scored a hat-trick for Rangers in the 1996 Scottish FA Cup final?

37. Dundee United beat Rangers in the 1994 Scottish FA Cup final. Who scored the only goal?

38. Who is Chelsea top all-time goalscorer?

39. Which player scored the extra-time winner in the 1985 FA Cup final?

40. In the 1970 FA Cup final replay between Chelsea and Leeds United who scored the winning goal?

41. In the 1973 FA Cup final Sunderland were shock 1-0 victors over Leeds United, who scored the only?

42. Who scored the 89th minute winner for Arsenal in their 3-2 win over Manchester United in the 1979 FA Cup final?

43. Who scored Arsenal's second goal at Anfield that won the 1988-89 League Championship?

44. Who scored the first goal in that match?

45. Which famous son scored twice in the 1989 League Cup final?

46. Which player has scored the most penalties for one club in a season?

47. **Which player saw his penalty saved by Nottingham Forest goalkeeper Mark Crossley in the 1991 FA Cup final?**

48. Which player scored in all four divisions of the Football League and the Premiership in his career?

49. **Which Premiership club scored four goals in four minutes against Southampton on 7 February 1993?**

50. In the 1995 Coca-Cola Cup final who scored Liverpool's two goals?

51. **In the 1995 FA Cup final who scored the only goal?**

52. Who was the leading goalscorer in Division One in 1995-6?

53. **Who was the leading goalscorer in Division Two in 1995-6?**

54. Who was the leading goalscorer in Division Three in 1995-6?

55. **Who was Chesterfield's top goalscorer in the 1995-6 season?**

56. How many goals did Neil Shipperley scored for Southampton in the 1995-6 season?

57. **Who was the leading goalscorer for Arsenal in the 1995-6 season?**

58. Which player has scored the most goals in total aggregate for one club?

59. **Which player has scored the most top-flight hat-tricks in a season since the war?**

60. Which player scored three consecutive hat-tricks in the old Division One?

61. Which Premiership player scored five hat-tricks in the 1995-6 season?

62. For the first time in the Premiership on September 23 1995 three hat-tricks were scored on the same day, who scored them?

63. Who was Liverpool's top goalscorer in the 1995-6 season?

64. Manchester City's top goalscorer in the 1995-6 season was Uwe Rosler, how many did he score?

65. Which player has scored the most goals in an international?

66. Who is the Republic of Ireland's top international goalscorer?

67. How many goals did Geoff Hurst score for England during his international career?

68. Who was the first player in British football to settle a match with the 'golden goal' sudden death decider?

69. Who scored the winning goal for Birmingham City against Carlisle in the Auto Windscreens Shield final of 1995?

70. Which club has had the highest goal scoring aggregate in the Premiership?

71. Who was Tottenham's top goalscorer in the 1995-6 season?

72. Terry Venables made two international appearances for England as a player, how many goals did he score?

73. How many goals has Stuart Pearce scored for England?

74. Who was West Ham's top goalscorer in the 1995-6 season?

75. Who is Celtic's top all-time goalscorer?

61. Alan Shearer 62. Tony Yeboah (Leeds), Alan Shearer (Blackburn), Robbie Fowler (Liverpool). **63. Robbie Fowler with 28.** 64. 9 **65. Vivian Woodward with 7 for England v France in an amateur international in November 1906.** 66. Frank Stapleton (1977-90) 20 goals in 71 games. **67. 24** 68. Iain Dunn (Huddersfield) on November 30 1994 in the Auto Windscreens Shield. **69. Paul Tait.** 70. Newcastle in 1993/94. **71. Teddy Sheringham with 16.** 72. None. **73. 5** 74. Tony Cottee with 10. **75. James McGrory (1922-39) with 397.**

76. Who is Rangers' top all-time goalscorer?

77. **Who was Liverpool's top goalscorer in their 1996 FA Cup run?**

78. Who is Liverpool's top all-time goalscorer?

79. **How many goals did Matthew Le Tissier score in the 1995/6 season?**

80. Who was Manchester City's top goalscorer in their 1995/6 FA Cup campaign?

81. **Who scored the goal in Nottingham Forest's 1-0 win over Malmo in the 1979 European Cup?**

82. In the 1976 UEFA Cup final 1st leg who scored Liverpool's three goals in their 3-2 win over Bruges?

83. **In the 2nd leg the score was 1-1 who scored Liverpool's goal?**

84. Which player has been Blackburn's highest scorer in a single season?

85. **Bolton Wanderers most capped player is also the club's top goalscorer, who is he?**

86. reston North End's most capped player is also the club's top goalscorer, who is he?

87. **Who has scored more goals for Portsmouth in a single season than any other player?**

88. Millwall's top all-time goalscorer scored 93 goals in total, who is he?

89. **Who is Manchester United's all-time top goalscorer?**

90. In the 1960/1 season one player scored 41 goals for Chelsea, a club record, who was he?

91. **Which aromatic striker has scored more goals for Aston Villa in a single season than any other?**

92. Which Championship winning Chelsea manager holds the record at Arsenal for being the top goalscorer in a single season?

93. **In Blackburn Rover's European Cup campaign of 1995/6 which player scored a hat-trick against Rosenborg?**

94. Everton beat Rapid Vienna 3-1 in the 1985 European Cup Winners Cup who scored Everton's goals?

95. **Who scored the goal in Wimbledon's historic 1-0 win over Liverpool in the 1988 FA Cup final?**

96. Who scored the winning 89th minute goal for Luton in their 3-2 Littlewoods Cup Final win over Arsenal in 1988?

97. **Who was the top scorer at Crystal Palace in the 1995-6 season?**

98. Which team on New Years Day 1996 scored 15 seconds from kick-off and again 15 seconds from the final whistle?

99. **Grimsby knocked West Ham out of the 1995-96 FA Cup in a 4th round replay, who scored Grimsby's goals in their 3-0 win?**

100. In the 1995/6 Division One Play-Off Final Leicester beat Crystal Palace 2-1, who were the goalscorers that day?

101. **Who scored the winning goal for Liverpool in their 1-0 win over Real Madrid in the 1981 European Cup?**

102. Geoff Hurst scored a hat-trick in the 1966 World Cup Final, who got the other one for England?

103. **Who scored the only goal in Nottingham Forest's 1-0 win over SV Hamburg in the 1980 European Cup?**

104. Who scored the equaliser for Leicester in the 1997 Coca-Cola Cup Final?

105. **Who scored the first goal for England under Terry Venables' reign?**

106. In the 1996 Anglo-Italian Cup Final Genoa beat Port Vale 5-2, Who scored the goals for Port Vale?

107. Who scored 414 goals for Chelsea, Tottenham and West Ham in just 591 matches?

108. Who won the Golden Boot for being Europe's leading league goalscorer in 1993?

109. Who scored twice for Liverpool against Nottinghan Forest in the 1989 FA Cup semi-final?

110. Who was Sunderland's top scorer in the 1994-95 season?

111. Since signing for Sheffield Wednesday in September 1992 this player has been the clubs top goalscorer three times, who is he?

112. Which Premiership striker did Newcastle buy for 15 million in August 1996?

113. Which Premiership striker did Liverpool buy for 8.5 million June 1995?

114. Which Premiership striker did Manchester United buy for 7 million in January 1995?

115. Who was Wimbledon's top goalscorer in the 1995-96 season?

116. Who is the all-time top league goalscorer for Wolves?

117. Who scored West Ham's goal in their 1-0 win over Arsenal in the 1980 FA Cup?

118. Who won the European Golden Boot in 1984?

119. In 1978 and 1979 which English striker was voted European Player of the Year?

120. Which striker was voted by the Football Writer's Association as their Player of the Year in 1968?

1. **Who was Arsenal's first scorer of the 1996-97 season?**

2. Which two players scored hat-tricks on the first day of the 1996-97 season?

3. **Who scored the first goal of the 1996-97 season?**

4. Which teams played in the first Sunday game of the 1996-97 season?

5. **In which game did Alan Shearer score his first goal for Newcastle?**

6. Which teams played in the only goalless draw on the opening day of the season?

7. **Who did Sunderland beat 4-1 away from home in their second game of the season?**

8. Which clubs beat Wimbledon in their three consecutive defeats at the start of the season?

9. **Who did Middlesborough beat 4-1 on September 4?**

10. Who inflicted the firstPremiership defeat of the season on Manchester United?

11. **How many games did Manchester United go unbeaten at the start of the season?**

12. Who did Wimbledon beat to record their first win of the season?

13. **Who scored a hat-trick in Southampton's 6-3 win over Manchester United?**

14. Who were two points clear at top of the Premiership after matches on November 2?

15. **Who did Blackburn beat 3-0 to record their first win of the season in their 12th game?**

12th TIME LUCKY

1. **John Hartson** 2. Kevin Campbell and Fabrizio Ravanelli 3. **Stig Inge Bjornebye** 4. Southampton and Chelsea 5. **His second against Wimbledon** 6. Sunderland and Leicester 7. **Nottingham Forest** 8. Manchester United, Newcastle and Leeds 9. **West Ham** 10. Newcastle, 5-0 11. 9 12. Tottenham 13. **Egil Ostenstadt** 14. Newcastle 15. Liverpool

16. Who scored a hat-trick in Everton's 7-1 win over Southampton in November?

17. **Who were beaten 2-0 by Arsenal on the opening day of the season?**

18. Which club inflicted Newcastle's first defeat of the season?

19. **Which team did West Ham beat for their first victory of the season?**

20. Against which team did Gianfranco Zola score his first goal for Chelsea?

21. **How many goals did Robbie Fowler score against Middlesborough when they met at Anfield in December?**

22. How many games had Wimbledon gone unbeaten before they lost 5-0 to Aston Villa?

23. **Who did Chelsea beat 2-0 on Boxing Day?**

24. Who did Manchester United beat 4-0 on Boxing Day?

25. **The game between which clubs was postponed on Boxing Day?**

26. How many goals did Les Ferdinand score in Newcastle's 7-1 win over Tottenham?

27. **Who scored the first goal of the New Year?**

28. 55,133 people turned out to see Manchester United play who on New Year's Day?

29. **How many goals had the Premiership's leading marksman Ian Wright scored by January 1?**

30. Which teams played in the first Sunday game of the New Year?

16. Gary Speed 17. **West Ham** 18. Everton 19. **Southampton** 20. Everton 21. 4 22. 14 games 23. **Aston Villa** 24. Nottingham Forest 25. **Wimbledon and West Ham** 26. 2 27. **Shearer, after 4 minutes** 28. Aston Villa 29. 23 30. Tottenham and Manchester United

31. **Who scored an own goal for Arsenal when they lost at Sunderland in January?**

32. Who scored two goals for Sheffield Wednesday when they lost 4-2 at Middlesborough?

33. **Which team were leading the Premiership into the New Year?**

34. Which team lifted themselves from the bottom of the table with a win on New Year's Day?

35. **Manchester United went to the top of the Premiership on January 29 for the first time with a win over who?**

36. Who did Liverpool beat 4-0 at home in February?

37. **Who scored a hat-trick in Leicester's 4-2 win over Derby in February?**

38. Who scored for both teams when Derby beat Chelsea 3-2 on March 1?

39. **Which team conceded two own goals in the first five minutes at Manchester United?**

40. Who scored a hat-trick against Sunderland in a 4-0 win in March?

41. **Which team conceded six against Middlesborough, including a hat-trick from Ravanelli, in March?**

42. Sunderland players scored all three goals in the Rokerites 2-1 win over who in March?

43. **Who scored Liverpool's 90th minute winner when they beat Newcastle 4-3?**

44. Who scored two goals for West Ham in their 3-2 home victory over Chelsea in March?

45. **Who scored a hat-trick in his club's 3-1 win over Wimbledon in March?**

46. How many players were on the scoresheet when Chelsea played Sunderland in March?

47. Who scored Derby's last minute winner in their 3-2 win over Chelsea in March?

48. Who scored the first Premiership hat-trick of the New Year?

49. Newcastle beat which team 4-0 in March, described as the best performance under Kenny Dalglish since he took over?

50. Dennis Bergkamp scored two goals for Arsenal against which club on March 8?

51. Which club beat Middlesborough 3-1 on March 1?

52. How many games did Manchester United lose between January 29 and March 29?

53. Who was Manchester United's first scorer of the season?

54. Who scored a first minute own goal when Tottenham lost 2-1 to Chelsea on February 1?

55. Who were the two players sent off on New Year's Day?

56. Who scored the last goal of the game when Tottenham lost 7-1 to Newcastle in December?

57. Which two teams played in the last game of 1996, when they met on December 29?

58. How many Premiership games were postponed on January 1?

59. Blackburn lost to two goals from which player in their opening game of the season?

60. Who was Everton's first scorer of the season?

61. **How many goals were scored in the nine games on the first day of the season?**

62. Niall Quinn scored two goals against which team in Sunderland's 4-1 victory in their second game of the season?

63. **Who scored Coventry's first goal of the season?**

64. Who were the four teams that Sheffield Wednesday beat in their first four games of the season?

65. **Which team ended Sheffield Wednesday's unbeaten Premiership run?**

66. Who scored an own goal for Leeds when they lost 4-0 to Manchester United in their fifth game of the season?

67. **Which team came back from a 1-0 half time deficit to beat Sheffield Wednesday 4-1 in September?**

68. Who scored the first goal when Newcastle beat Mancheter United 5-0?

69. **How many points did Blackburn have after their first 11 games of the season?**

70. Who scored Chelsea's only goal when they were beaten 5-1 by Liverpool in September?

71. **Who scored Manchester United's goals when they lost 6-3 to Southampton?**

72. What was the score of the Merseyside derby at Anfield?

73. **Who scored Southampton's only goal when they lost 7-1 to Everton?**

74. What was the score in the North London derby at Highbury in November?

75. **Against which club did Ian Rush score his first Premiership goal for Leeds?**

76. What was the score when Arsenal and Newcastle met at St James' Park on November 30?

77. **What was the score when West Ham played Manchester United at Upton Park in December?**

78. Who did Manchester United beat 5-0 on December 21?

79. **What was the score when Liverpool met Newcastle in the last Premiership game before Christmas?**

80. Against which team did Darren Huckerby score his first goal for Coventry since his move from Newcastle?

81. **Who scored the last Premiership goal of 1996?**

82. Which team did Chelsea beat 1-0 to make a winning start to 1997?

83. **Who was the first person of the season to be sent off?**

84. Which three teams won 4-0 on September 6, when they played Leeds, Coventry and Everton, respectively?

85. **Against which team did Patrick Berger score his first goal for Liverpool?**

86. Liverpool scored two goals in two minutes when they beat Newcastle 4-3. Who scored them?

87. **Who scored Newcastle's third goal in their 4-3 loss at Anfield?**

88. Who scored twice for Blackburn when they beat Liverpool 3-0 at Ewood in November?

89. **Against which team did Ruud Gullit score his only Premiership goal of the season?**

90. Middlesborough's foreigners Ravanelli, Festa, Emerson and Juninho all scored in their game against which team?

1. **Who scored Marseille's winning goal in the 1993 European Cup Final?**

2. Who was the World Footballer of the Year in 1994?

3. **Which two 1999-97 Chelsea players played in the 1989 European Cup final?**

4. Which player became the first man to win the European Cup with two different clubs?

5. **Who was the first Englishman to be voted European Footballer of the Year?**

6. What year was it?

7. **Who is the last player to win both PFA Player of the Year and Young Player of the Year in the same season?**

8. What year was it?

9. **Who was the first player to twice be voted European Footballer of the Year?**

10. Who is the only goalkeeper, so far, to win the European Footballer of the year award?

11. **Which nationality was he?**

12. Who beat Alan Shearer to the World Footballer of the Year award in 1997?

13. **How many Manchester United players have been voted European Footballer of the Year?**

14. Who became the first non-European to win the European Footballer of the Year?

15. **Who was the last player to be the European Footballer of the Year for three consecutive years?**

16. How many times has Johan Cruyff won the European Footballer of the Year title?

17. **Who became the first Bulgarian to be voted European Footballer of the Year?**

18. Who was the last English player to be European Footballer of the Year?

19. **And what year was it?**

20. Who was the last Russian player to be European Footballer of the Year?

21. **What year was it?**

22. Which Danish player was voted European Footballer of the Year in 1977?

23. **Which European team were voted World Team of the Year in 1987?**

24. Which English manager was voted World Manager of the Year in 1985?

25. **Which German has conceded a penalty in both an European Cup Final and World Cup Final?**

26. Which Italian club did Brazilian Zico play for?

27. **Which Scottish manager was voted World Manager of the Year in 1993?**

28. At which club was Kevin Keegan at when he won the European Footballer of the Year awards?

29. **Which European Footballer of the Year missed a penalty in a World Cup Final penalty shoot-out?**

30. Which Russian player was voted 1975 European Footballer of the Year?